T5-CAJ-541

Nellie Brown, or The Jealous Wife, with Other Sketches

Blacks in the American West

EDITORS

Richard Newman

Marcia Renée Sawyer

The involvement of blacks at every point in the exploration, history, and ongoing life of the American West remains a little-known story. The books—both fiction and nonfiction—in this series aim to preserve these stories and to celebrate the achievement and culture of early African-American westerners.

NELLIE BROWN

OR

THE JEALOUS WIFE,

WITH

OTHER SKETCHES

THOMAS DETTER

"This work is perfectly chaste and moral in every particular"

Introduction by Frances Smith Foster

University of Nebraska Press
Lincoln and London

Originally self-published in 1871 in San Francisco.

Manufactured in the United States of America

∞The paper in this book meets the minimum requirements of American National Standard for Information Sciences—Permanence of Paper for Printed Library Materials, ANSI Z39.48-1984.

Library of Congress Cataloging-in-Publication Data
Detter, Thomas, b. ca. 1826.
Nellie Brown, or, The jealous wife : with other sketches / Thomas Detter ; introduction by Frances Smith Foster.
p. cm.—(Blacks in the American West)
Originally published: San Francisco : Cuddy & Hughes, printers, 1871.
Includes bibliographical references (p.).
ISBN 0-8032-1704-8 (alk. paper)
1. Afro-Americans—West (U.S.)—Social life and customs—Fiction.
I. Title. II. Series.
PS1536.D47N45 1996
813'.4—dc20
96-1023
CIP

Contents

Introduction

Nellie Brown, or The Jealous Wife, with Other Sketches was published in 1871 by Thomas Detter, an African American who was a frontier businessman and gold miner, a civil rights leader, and a Methodist minister. "Nellie Brown, or The Jealous Wife" is a novella about the misadventures that occur when a woman's husband's visit to her best friend is misinterpreted. When this story was published, domestic fiction was very popular; however, it was a genre dominated by white women writers and one that generally ended with marriage as the happy-ever-after reward for virtue, sincerity, and good manners. This story, then, is unusual for its subject matter and its author. The "Other Sketches" are shorter but no less provocative. "The Octoroon Slave of Cuba" provides an unusual alternative to "tragic mulatto" fiction such as William Wells Brown's *Clotel.* "Uncle Joe" is an adaptation of an African-American folktale that resembles the later work by Charles W. Chesnutt. The essays are personal and opinionated but insightful and useful to readers then and now. Whether he is predicting the future prospects of "Idaho City," describing the impact of the "Central Pacific Railroad," or reporting a painful instance of racial discrimination during "My Trip to Baltimore," Detter was writing to inform and to inspire his readers. Today, *Nellie Brown, or The Jealous Wife, with Other Sketches* has the dual attraction of being interesting in both art and artifact. The book brings together fiction and essays set in antebellum Virginia and Maryland, Louisiana, Cuba, Idaho, and California but published in San Francisco by a resident of Elko, Nevada. In so doing, it illustrates the unity and diversity of effort in the creation of these United States even as it challenges our ideas of history, literature, and the ways in which we might read both.

Detter and his writings have languished in dusky archives for almost a century. Their obscurity stems less from any inherent defects in the text or insignificance of the writer than from social, political, and academic traditions that have worked to exclude, ignore, or demean the lives and letters of those outside the Anglo-American male mainstream. Historiography, whether literary or social, demands the selection and presentation of information according to particular criteria. Historians have never been required to include the achievements of all individuals, regardless of their fame or influence. History favors those presidents and moguls, pirates and popes, dreamers and schemers whose lives and contributions are truly exceptional or reflect a communal story exceptionally well. Although a few African Americans have made the pages of some history tomes and Frederick Douglass, Sojourner Truth, Nat Love, and Harriet Tubman have joined Marilyn Monroe and Elvis Presley as "exceptional" lives worthy of their own postage stamps, until recently traditional methodology and criteria routinely eliminated virtually all women and people of color from academic or popular depictions of history.

It is shameful, however, that writers such as Thomas Detter have been allowed to disappear almost without a trace and certainly without the benefit of historical and aesthetic evaluations based on the objective standards so often proposed but rarely practiced. Thus, this republication of *Nellie Brown, or The Jealous Wife, with Other Sketches* has at least two purposes. It offers a collection of stories and essays that are entertaining and informative, and it presents another candidate for inclusion in a revised history of American culture. There is no doubt that Thomas Detter's words had significant impact on the development of western African America. You are invited to consider this text within its context and judge for yourself its value as art and artifact. This republication is part of what is proving to be yet another Reconstruction Era in the United States, a reconstruction of American cultural history to portray and encourage a wider range of contributions from a larger percentage of its peoples. The move toward such revisionist or inclusive scholarship became obvious in the 1970s and flourished in the 1980s. But as we look toward the twenty-first century, now is a particularly advantageous time to become acquainted with some of the writings of a nineteenth-century visionary whose concerns are so remarkably similar to our current ones.

Mid-nineteenth-century America was—as late-twentieth-century America is now—in transition, socially, politically, economically, and theologically. California and the Northwest territories were particularly important sites of conflicting interpretations of similar dreams. The discovery of silver and gold and the building of the railroads precipitated a rush by people of all races and creeds to settle this region. Displaced dominants fleeing Reconstruction politics in the East were met by the formerly oppressed, who were determined to design even more democratic governments in the West. Prejudice and discrimination against Mexicans, Chinese, Native Americans, and others were rampant among Anglo-Americans. But tolerance is not genetic and a common enemy does not ensure coalitions of the oppressed. Protestant blacks criticized Catholic browns and both condemned Chinese and Jews as heathens. Irish immigrants declined to work with Native Americans. All in all, the Promised Land was also the Problematic Land as each element vied to build communities shaped by varying past experiences and modeled on conflicting plans for the future. Nonetheless, for many African Americans the Far West was their best bet for freedom and prosperity. Some became quite wealthy. Blacks were an estimated one percent of the gold rushers, but in 1855 those in California reportedly had property worth over $3.5 million. Wealth was no more evenly distributed within the black communities than it was in any others. Not everyone who went to California succeeded, and many of those who acquired wealth were not able to keep it. Especially the illiterate, unskilled former slaves, but also many freeborn urbanites unused to frontier law, lacked the prerequisite practical knowledge, economic sophistication, and political acumen. Still, African Americans fought for their rights and security using as much of the political, civic, and religious systems as possible. They also formed very strong and aggressive organizations of their own, including a western line of the Underground Railroad. Certain members of the African-American community were quick to inform newly arrived slaves of their legal status and to encourage black emigrants to become educated and participating citizens. One writer described them as "especially talented" in liberating their enslaved brothers and sisters and devoting "a great deal of energy and intelligence" to that end (quoted in Lapp). Among the better-known activists were Mary Ellen Pleasant, the wealthy and influential former slave who sued against discrimination on San Francisco streetcars and helped finance John Brown's campaign at Harper's Ferry; poet James M. Whitfield, author of *America, and Other Poems* (1853) and editor of the procolonization publication *African American Repository*; Mifflin W. Gibbs, the merchant and miner who, disgusted with California's racism, led a group to British Columbia and became a city council member in the predominately white James Bay district before returning to the United States to practice law; Jeremiah B. Sanderson, educator and abolitionist, African Methodist Episcopal minister and fundraiser for black Union soldiers; and Thomas Detter.

Although he was one of the petitioners to Congress to aid African Americans in leaving the United States for more hospitable countries, Detter did not join his friend Mifflin W. Gibbs in organizing African-American emigration to Canada. Thomas Detter placed his energies into making the U.S. Constitution work for all U.S. citizens and trying to realize the American Dream of economic well-being and social productivity. Detter believed in the potential of the mining business and traveled extensively throughout the Northwest pursuing opportunities that mining afforded. He may have attempted some prospecting himself, but generally he exploited entrepreneurial opportunities in the service sector, plying his trade as a barber, selling his patented cough syrups and hair restoratives, and otherwise investing in the various economic opportunities associated with new settlements. Apparently Detter's activities earned him a fair degree of economic comfort and social prestige. His 1876 marriage to Emily Brinson was reported in both the *Pacific Appeal* and the *Eureka Sentinel* on 18 November. The reports referred to him as Doctor Thomas Detter, "the wellknown proprietor of the Silver Brick shaving saloon and bathing establishment," and reported that their wedding reception was "attended by nearly all of the colored folk in town, besides some twenty-five or thirty white people, including some of our most prominent citizens and their wives."

Thomas Detter's success did not come at the cost of his racial and civic activism. Wherever he went, Detter took leadership roles in African-American religious and political organizations, spoke at rallies, and agitated for equal rights. By 1864 he was already known as "one of the old wheelhorses" of the California equal rights movement. One of the first crusades he joined was for the abolition of the ban against blacks testifying in court cases that involved whites. When he moved to Nevada, he continued the campaign. It was a long and frustrating battle, but by 1870 Detter and his cohorts had won the right to testify in court and Thomas Detter, James M. Whitfield, and two other black Nevadans had served on a jury in an Elko County civil case.

When he published *Nellie Brown, or The Jealous Wife, with Other Sketches*, Thomas Detter was about forty years old and living in the isolated frontier settlement of Elko, Nevada. Detter was not, however, an amateur writer or a rural sage. By 1871 his reputation as a correspondent for the *San Francisco Elevator* and the *Pacific Appeal* had been established for at least a decade. In his history of African Americans in Nevada, Elmer R. Rusco says that "Thomas Detter was the most articulate of the remarkable blacks who lived in nineteenth-century Nevada and one of the most articulate in the West. Probably only editors Philip Bell and Peter Anderson left a more complete record of their ideas" (104). Newspaper articles by and about Thomas Detter make it fairly easy to outline his life between 1852 and 1880, but the years before and after remain something of a mystery. Detter was born into a free middle-class family around 1826 in Maryland or Washington DC. His father was a stonemason and property owner whose 1840 will left his wife, Eleanor, and their two children, Thomas and Martha, a house and other property and decreed that Thomas be apprenticed as a shoemaker until he reached twenty-one years of age. Like other African Americans, including the son and brother of Harriet Jacobs (author of *Incidents in the Life of a Slave Girl*), young Detter migrated to California, in Rusco's words, "looking to the sunny side of life and for glittering gold" (9). He arrived in San Francisco on the steamer *John L. Stephens* in 1852 and within three years had achieved such respect within the African-American community that along with Jeremiah B. Sanderson he was elected a Sacramento County delegate to the first Colored Citizens of the State of California Convention. Detter served on the State Executive Committee of that convention for two or three years before leaving for Idaho and Washington Territories. Detter traveled extensively in the Northwest territories but returned to San Francisco regularly. In 1860, on one of those returns, he married. Little is known of his first wife: her name was Caroline, she was born in Maryland and raised in Philadelphia, and she arrived in San Francisco in 1855 and died there in 1874. Detter lived in mining camps and settlements throughout the Northwest Territories, where he helped found African-American communities by advertising the status and prospects of new gold or silver mines, describing the towns cropping up in response to the expansion of railroads, and agitating for schools, votes, jobs, and justice for blacks who settled in those places. His newspaper reports generally emphasized the grand natural beauty and economic opportunities, with emphasis on the abundant rewards for courage, persistence, and optimism. Writing from Idaho City in 1868, he said that "a mountain life is indeed romantic, as well as novel, its best times are always ahead."

Searching for the best times ahead, Thomas Detter left Elko shortly after publishing his book. The year 1874 found him in Eureka, Nevada, where political and personal events sorely tested his optimism. His wife died in February, his son died in May, and in November of that year the Republican failure to pass the Civil Rights bill forced him to abandon the party in which he had so strongly believed and for which he had campaigned assiduously. Detter's faith in the Republicans died, but not his belief in the American political system. He continued to urge African Americans to vote and to demand accountability from their elected officials. "Let us vote for no candidate who believes a white American citizen is entitled to more privileges and consideration than a colored citizen," he declared in one of his *Pacific Appeal* articles (24 October 1874).

In 1880 Thomas Detter reportedly participated in an organizational meeting of African-American residents of Eureka, Nevada, but the details are vague, and after that year his name seems to have been lost to public record. Elmer R. Rusco, probably the foremost authority on Detter's life, speculates that the economic decline in Eureka in the mid-1880s probably forced Detter to relocate. Rusco also reports that "a search of the cemeteries at Eureka did not reveal any markers for himself or his family, although presumably his son was buried in Eureka. The condition of the cemeteries is such that many graves remain unidentified, however" (162).

Though his origins and his fate remain to be unveiled by others, the text and context of Thomas Detter's *Nellie Brown, or The Jealous Wife, with Other Sketches* are more readily perceptible. The book promoted particular moral values and commitments while providing wholesome entertainment. In this dual purpose, Detter's text is within the mainstream of nineteenth-century American literary production. American literature has traditionally assumed the difficult task of providing both instruction and diversion. With the readers' willing suspension of disbelief, books were (and generally still are) expected to transport them to worlds of imagination far beyond the ordinary and often stressful realities of their daily lives. Books were expected not only to be windows on the world, but they were to become worlds within which readers could vicariously experience times long ago, places far away, peril without pain, or beauty that lasts forever. At the same time, if reading were to be a worthwhile activity, it had to be productive, it had to account for something. Literature had to convey, if not the best thoughts of the best minds, then at least a truth worth the telling. Fiction, especially, was judged by the values and morals that it promulgated.

Thomas Detter was neither the first nor the only African-American writer to harness the literary muse to cultivate pragmatic, even overtly political, fields. In 1852 Frederick Douglass conscripted the novella form into the service of abolition with "The Heroic Slave." William Wells Brown's drama, *The Escape, or a Leap for Freedom* (1858) is an early example of propagandist theater. Frances Ellen Watkins Harper's short story "The Two Offers" (1859), her dramatic poem *Moses, a Story of the Nile* (c. 1868), and her novel *Minnie's Sacrifice* (1869) are other earlier examples of subverting conventionally Anglo-American literary means to African-American ends.

Most readers familiar with such nineteenth-century African-American texts will recognize that Thomas Detter's use of "writing as fighting" is squarely within the African-American literary arena. Those who may be surprised that racial equality is not the central issue in *Nellie Brown, or The Jealous Wife, with Other Sketches* might recall two things. First, although "Nellie Brown" is the title story of the volume, "My Trip to Baltimore" and "Give the Negro a Chance" are also a part of that collection. Second, Thomas Detter lived and worked on the western frontier. The same kind of adventurous or rebellious spirit that drove settlers to the frontier and particularly to the mining camps put traditional family values at risk. The highly disproportionate number of men clearly threatened the wedlock ideal. Despite the animosity or competition that flourished among the various cultural groups, the exposure to other cultural traditions and religious attitudes encouraged social experimentation. Although civil rights was certainly an important issue in western African America and claimed much of Detter's time and thought, racial equality was not always the most immediately pressing concern. In 1871, when *Nellie Brown, or The Jealous Wife, with Other Sketches* appeared, Thomas Detter, a minister, politician, and businessman, a husband and a father, felt that those building the postbellum nation were targeted by myriad arrows.

Another question might arise from the story's setting in Virginia and its use of white protagonists who are in fact racist and slaveholders. Part of the reason for these elements has to do with the genre with which Detter was experimenting; this topic is discussed more fully below. Another part, though, is African-American writers' familiarity with and attraction to style as well as substance. Many delighted in exploring the practical possibilities of literary forms such as the sonnet, the epic, the religious narrative, and the sentimental novel. One way in which Detter's novella subverts the plantation fiction tradition that obviously influenced its form is with the white characters' display of a range of attitudes toward blacks and slavery. Those attitudes often are the major means of making otherwise flat characterizations interesting. The depiction of the widow's purity, piety, and domesticity is complicated by her inability to deal with Nan and her repeated rapid transformations from name-calling, foot-stamping shrew to gracious and genteel Southern belle. In the same vein, the exchange with Nellie Brown when Sue asks her for free papers exposes the limits of Nellie's relatively liberal racial attitudes and reveals the shrewd self-preservation that underlies Sue's antics.

The book is interesting to literary production outside the African-American tradition because two of its fiction pieces are among the earliest examples of American divorce fiction. Yet the practice of segregated literary study has prevented acknowledgment of this even as scholars have needed the evidence of just such texts to trace the genre's development.

Although there is some disagreement over who first published fiction focusing on divorce, James Harwood Barnett's *Divorce and the American Divorce Novel, 1858–1937* identifies T. S. Arthur's *The Hand but Not the Heart* (1858) as a likely candidate for that honor. Like Detter's "Nellie Brown, or The Jealous Wife," Arthur's fiction is not so much a condemnation of divorce as it is a demonstration, in Barnett's words, that "improper marriages, jealousy, and remarriage after divorce [lead] to unfortunate consequences" (71). T. S. Arthur and Thomas Detter extended and modified the popular sentimental fiction form past the happy-ever-after endings that had ignored the increasing incidence of divorce in antebellum and postbellum United States.

Barnett is just one of those whose research has revised our notions of romance and marriage in the good old days by demonstrating that divorce is as American as apple pie. In *Divorce: An American Tradition*, for example, Glenda Riley notes that a Puritan court granted the first American couple their decree in 1639. From statistical evidence of increased divorce cases in the post–Revolutionary War period, Martin Schultz offers the theory that "the spirit of political independence fostered modern values, such as personal freedom, equality, and a concern for the future" (512). During that period divorces were particularly common in states such as Rhode Island, Connecticut, Vermont, Maine, Pennsylvania, Ohio, South Dakota, and Utah. After 1850 Indiana was sometimes referred to as "a divorce mecca, churning out easy divorces to people from stricter states with little regard for long-term consequences to spouses and children" (Riley 63).

According to Barnett's study, divorce was "relatively com mon" by the 1840s and "alarmingly so" in the 1860s. "The divorce theme entered the American novel about the time the country became concerned with increasing divorce" and before legislative initiatives against divorce flourished. Barnett reminds us that reaction against divorce "began after the Civil War . . . and may be regarded as a part of the general reform movement which occurred in the post-war decades in municipal government, civil services, housing and other spheres of social life" (135–36). As Barnett and numerous other scholars have indicated, Reconstruction's concern with citizenship and suffrage was not limited to race. Even those middle-class white women whose move from hearths and nurseries to field and factory had been necessitated by Johnny's marching off to war had something to say about their roles within the reconstructed families. They were reading Elizabeth Cady Stanton, listening to Anna Julia Cooper, and joining Frances E. Willard in picketing saloons rather than feeding and favoring their fathers, husbands, and sons.

That Thomas Detter intended the novella "Nellie Brown, or The Jealous Wife" as the primary focus in his collection is clear from the volume's title, from the proportion of the book devoted to this narrative (its 118 pages comprise about two thirds of the text), and from the introduction. Detter describes his intent in terms that specifically relate to the title story. "The design of this work," Detter says, "is to show the unhappy results of jealousy and misplaced confidence, and the wicked designs of corrupt parties." This statement can be read as relevant to the overall collection, because each sketch demonstrates the necessity for, or celebrates the triumph of, faith, hope, and charity. However, the next sentences relate specifically to "Nellie Brown": "Man and woman were created for a noble purpose by their Creator;" Detter writes, "but how often do we see families that have lived long happily together rent in twain by such malignant characters as Mrs. H., Aunt Polly and Martha Lovejoy—more fully explained in the following work."

In naming these three women as the villains, Detter declares their primacy to our understanding of his narrative. Each of the other characters bears some responsibility for the events that transpire, but theirs are primarily lapses of good judgment or self-discipline. The three women, however, are guilty of deliberately destructive behavior. They are repeatedly identified as divorced women, and their activities are compared to the foxes that helped Samson burn down his neighbors' fields. (Samson's motive was also related to marital discord, adultery, and deceit; see Judges 14–15). "All communities," Detter admonishes, include "malicious persons" who will destroy the very fabric of society if they succumb to jealousy and are left to run amok. Detter's introductory paragraph and particularly his statement that "Man and woman were created for a noble purpose," which precedes his warning against those who deliberately attack the family circle, could be interpreted as a definition of marriage as a divinely ordained institution and a subsequent rejection of divorce.

When one reads the next story, "The Octoroon Slave of Cuba," that interpretation becomes complicated. When Jane Gray discovers her husband is a fraud and a fornicator, she divorces him and requires him to marry the mother of his children. Marriage, Jane Gray says, is "a civil contract between the parties." When its duties are violated, it is the obligation of the injured party to seek redress. By her actions, she demonstrates that the injured party does not require any outside authorization to do so; Jane terminates her marriage herself. "I, this day, decree my own divorce. Whether censured or sustained by public sentiment—I care not," she stated.

A story that affirms marriage and divorce as personal or civil matters hearkens back to the earlier and more liberal traditions of colonial America and thereby becomes a dissident, radical voice in the post–Civil War version of a Contract with America. Stories that move beyond the happy-ever-after endings so prolific in mid-nineteenth-century tales were both politically and artistically on the cutting edge. As Joseph Allen Boone has argued in *Tradition Counter Tradition: Love and the Form of Fiction*, "the marital ideal serves as a metonymy for proper social order" (7). Even Mrs. E. D. E. N. Southworth, who is considered another pioneer in this genre, characterized marriage as "the most sacred tie on earth" because it secures not only "the peace of families, [but] the social welfare of the whole community." Divorce fiction such as Detter's had serious social significance, for as a genre it not only demonstrated that marriage as the happy ending is merely the end of one of life's chapters but also tended to attack the forces that threatened the matrimonial knot more than to condemn divorce itself.

As divorce fiction, "Nellie Brown" and "The Octoroon Slave of Cuba" both underscore and undermine conventional literary scholarship. "Nellie Brown," for example, fits the third pattern of the wedlock or domestic plot that Boone characterizes: "initially troubled spouses generally undergo a series of misfortunes and threats analogous to those occurring in the courtship narrative before reuniting happily" (10). And like much of the fiction in Barnett's study, Detter's melodramatic plots, flat characters, and long dissertations on the social and moral implications of these individuals' experiences invite readers to ponder the issues rather than identify with the actors or their actions. Divorce is a central concern, but the text is more concerned with assailing improper marriages, jealousy, and remarriage after divorce than it is with the propriety of divorce itself.

Thomas Detter's "Nellie Brown" is exactly the missing link that James Harwood Barnett needed for his history of divorce fiction. Having identified the beginnings in 1858, he has little evidence beyond two novels and a few short stories by T. S. Arthur, a play by Augustin Daly, and suspected periodical fiction by E. D. E. N. Southworth before the publication of William Dean Howells's *A Modern Instance* in 1881. Barnett frets over the "time lag of ten to twenty years between the general concern over divorce (1860–1875) and reflection of this in a series of divorce novels as in the 1880's" but concludes that "the period from 1870 to 1881 appears to be barren of divorce novels and possibly of plays and dramas as well" (81). Barnett, like virtually all literary scholars prior to the 1960s, had confined his research to Anglo-American writers. Therefore, he did not know that Thomas Detter's "Nellie Brown, or The Jealous Wife" and "The Octoroon Slave of Cuba" disprove at least his 1870 date and provide the missing links he sought for his theory of the evolution of that genre.

Some parts of the collection by Thomas Detter are more compelling than others, but the book was issued as a collection and, with due regard for its context, it should be read and interpreted that way. Reading "Nellie Brown" alone encourages a different understanding than might follow "The Octoroon Slave of Cuba." Considering "Uncle Joe" in relation to Sue of "Nellie Brown" or the narrator of "My Trip to Baltimore" makes Detter's use of literary techniques such as irony and insinuation more obvious. References to Crispus Attucks and Daniel O'Connell in "Progress of America" take on new implications when read before "Boise City."

Thomas Detter's book certainly challenges how most of us imagine the United States as it approached its second century. The

Civil War looms so large that the mid–nineteenth century is generally spoken of as "antebellum" or "postbellum." When we think of westward expansion, quite often our mental eyes move across the plains watching the contest between Anglo-American pioneers and the Native Americans who resisted them, or focus on the annexation of Mexico, unless the sparkle of the Pacific Ocean and the glitter of gold remind us of California. Few gaze northward toward the settlers in Utah, Nevada, Idaho, Washington, and Oregon, but when they do, they see cowboys, gold miners, fur trappers, lumberjacks, padres, and exhausted pioneers peopling the Pacific Northwest. Writers, artists, intellectuals, politicians, and Protestant ministers are generally considered products of the northeastern states. Some acknowledge that writers such as Mark Twain, Bret Harte, Stephen Crane, and even Helen Hunt Jackson followed John Soule's advice to "Go west, young man," and honed their skills as journalists, fiction writers, and cultural historians. Yet theories and thoughts on American culture, and particularly on its literature, generally start at the Atlantic seaboard and stop abruptly at the Mississippi River. *Nellie Brown, or The Jealous Wife, with Other Sketches*, however, is a book produced in the Northwest that deliberately enters the conversation and employs literary conventions that would seem to be exclusively eastern. In so doing, it reminds us now, as it did readers then, that cultural aspirations and production, intellectual and political concerns, and economic and social mores were no more geographically restricted then than they are now.

Nellie Brown, or The Jealous Wife, with Other Sketches has been described as the "first known book of fiction authored by a black person in the West." This definition is a bit problematic for at least three reasons. First, it is not exclusively a work of fiction: the three works of fiction, especially the brief novella highlighted in the title, are entertaining and engaging, but the book also contains six essays that are interesting and instructive in their own right. Second, although Detter's book appears to be the earliest extant text published west of the Mississippi River by an African American, both it and its author have been routinely omitted from most accounts of African-American literary history, its existence known only to a few scholars, and its pages unavailable to twentieth-century readers generally. Thus, the extent to which this is a "known" work is minimal. Finally, the emphasis on the author's race, location, and precociousness diverts attention from the entertaining qualities and larger literary contexts of this book. Although identifiable elements that place Detter's work within the categories of African-American literature and western American literature, its subject matter, form, and function are also similar to, and representative of, American literature in general.

Today's readers will find much the same enjoyment in this book as they do in other mid-nineteenth-century literature. Here are stories of melodrama, revenge, mystery, intrigue, optimism, sentimentality, and chaste sensuality. Here are essays that effusively celebrate industrialization, capitalism, and education as the tools with which the American Dream should be reconstructed. Readers will be intrigued to find familiar names, events, and philosophies in contexts and applications with which they are generally unfamiliar. They will also be challenged, chagrined, and perhaps confused, angered, or embarrassed. For *Nellie Brown, or The Jealous Wife, with Other Sketches* was written not only to delight and to instruct but also to confront and to change. Detter's ends and his means may jar our assumptions about African Americans, family values, literary functions, and other aspects of our past and our present. All in all, I wager that even a quick perusal of this book will demonstrate once more that the United States is indeed a country of one from many and can add to our developing understanding and appreciation of its diversity. The rediscovery of this work could be to contemporary American studies what the discovery of gold was to the development of the American West.

Frances Smith Foster
Emory University

BIBLIOGRAPHY

Barnett, James Harwood. *Divorce and the American Divorce Novel 1858–1937: A Study in Literary Reflections of Social Influences.* 1939. Reprint, New York: Russell & Russell, 1968.

Beasley, Delilah. *The Negro Trail Blazers of California.* Los Angeles: Times-Mirror Printing and Binding House, 1919. Reprint, New York: Negro Universities Press, 1969.

Boone, Joseph Allen. *Tradition Counter Tradition: Love and the Form of Fiction.* Chicago: University of Chicago Press, 1987.

Lapp, Rudolph M. "Negro Rights Activities in Gold Rush California." *California Historical Society Quarterly* 65, no. 1 (March 1966) : 3–20.

Riley, Glenda. *Divorce: An American Tradition*. New York: Oxford University Press, 1991.

Rusco, Elmer R. *"Good Time Coming?" Black Nevadans in the Nineteenth Century.* Westport CT: Greenwood Press, 1975.

Schultz, Martin. "Divorce in Early America: Origins and Trends in Three North Central States." *Sociological Quarterly* 25, no. 4 (autumn 1984) : 511–25.

Nellie Brown, or The Jealous Wife, with Other Sketches

Introduction

Readers—The design of this work is to show the unhappy results of jealousy and misplaced confidence, and the wicked designs of corrupt parties. Man and woman were created for a noble purpose by their Creator; but how often do we see families that have lived long happily together rent in twain by such malignant characters as Mrs. H., Aunt Polly and Martha Lovejoy—more fully explained in the following work. Such characters are to be found in all communities, like hungry wolves hunting down their prey; they often paralyze the hopes of the good and just, cause doubts, gloom and despair to overhang their pathway, where the radiant sunlight of happiness had long beamed. Malicious persons, like Sampson's [sic] foxes, are ever scattering the firebrands of hate, mischief and discord, and should be shunned by all lovers of good society.

I ought to apologize for attempting to put this work before the public. I am entirely responsible for it. They are my own ideas, however crude they may be. Knowing that the works of the ablest writers are subject to the severest criticism, I put this book before the public to live or die upon its own merits. I was raised in the District of Columbia, where the education of colored persons was very limited. This work is perfectly chaste and moral in every particular. Hoping that it will receive a fair and impartial perusal, I remain, dear readers,

Your obedient servant,
The Author.

1. Nellie Brown, or The Jealous Wife

CHAPTER I

In the town of N——— resided H. Montgomery, a graduate of the Columbia College, Washington, D.C. He was prepossessing in appearance, easy manners, a social companion. By ardent study he became one of the first lawyers of Virginia; he seldom indulged in ornamentations at the bar; he was practical, logical, and stern; when aroused with the lash of sarcasm by his opponents, it was then resolves fired his breast, and the gleen of battle lit up his countenance. He never was known to retreat in the struggles for right, ever advancing with the shield of truth, and with the sword of justice cut his way through the ranks of his enemies, and invariably disarranged their plans, defeated their aims, and won laurels of victory. If oratory means the power to present thoughts, to hold an audience, to win favorable decisions for clients, *he* was indeed an orator. His ripe scholarship, concise and pointed arguments, caused his fame to spread far and wide. He kindled the fire of enthusiasm wherever he touched the public mind; he selected the purest ores of truth and the brightest gems of thought; he never engaged the enemy without being thoroughly equipped for the fight; he knew no fears; nothing swerved him from duty; honest and frank with his clients on all matters pertaining to business.

His associates in law, though jealous of his success, acknowledged his talents and abilities as a counsellor.

One of his happiest efforts was a divorce case, in which he was engaged as a counsellor in behalf of the defendant, Mr. B———.

He was accused of infidelity by his wife, to whom he had been married twelve long years. The fruit of that marriage was a girl and a boy, Maggie and Willie. They were just old enough to know a mother's love and a father's care. Peace and happiness had long dwelt in the cottage situated at the base of the mountain in old Virginia, surrounded with shrubbery and vines.

Mr. B. was a large cattle-dealer; his business required his absence from home for weeks; his wife, though amiable and loving, was not free from the sting of jealousy, and not slow in temper when aroused. Living at a mile distant from Mrs. B.'s farm, resided a prime Widow, who had not passed thirty summers, full of life, glee, and apparent happiness; with, perhaps, an exception, she felt the loss of her companion, who had shared her joys and woes during his life. Mr. B. and his wife felt deeply interested in her behalf; she was left upon the cold charities of a heartless world.

During Mr. B.'s absence from home the Widow visited Mrs. B. for weeks; they became the confidants of each other. So strong was their attachment, one would suppose them to be sisters.

Mrs. H., a woman who became jealous of the association of the widow and Mrs. B., was a person who did not hesitate to avenge herself upon her neighbors to gratify her personal prejudices.

Mr. B., on returning home, frequently stopped at the Widow's; her house was situated on the main road, which he had to pass.

It was in the month of July, and the meridian of day shone in its beauty and strength. The heat was intense; the feathered songsters, that had sang so sweetly as the orb of day rose o'er the Eastern slopes, had ceased their warblings and had taken shelter among the leaves of the trees. It was now about noon; the Widow was seated at the parlor window, embroidering a handkerchief. She heard the clattering of a horse's hoofs coming from the village—Greenbriar. Her heart leaped with joy; she said: "Can it be Mr. B. and Queen?" which was the name of the proud filly he rode.

The Widow arose from her seat and hastened to the door; much to her joy and delight it was Queen and her master. They seemed equally delighted to look upon the young Widow again; they seldom passed without halting. As Mr. B. rode up, the Widow said:

"I am delighted to see you; do alight and walk in."

After conversing a few moments, Mr. B. asked:

"When did you last hear from Nellie and the babies?"

"Dear me, I have just returned from your house yesterday; your wife and children are enjoying excellent health, and are over-anxious to see you."

"Yes," replied Mr. B. with a smile, "if I continue to roam around, as I have this last three weeks, those little *toads* will not know who their daddy is."

"They are continually prattling about Pa. It is just three weeks to-day, is it not, since you left home?" asked the Widow.

"It is," replied Mr. B., "and much longer than I intended to have stayed."

"Come in and rest yourself. Poor Queen looks as though she was tryed."

"We have come thirty-five miles from the village since seven o'clock. What time of day is it?"

"Go, Nan, in the dining-room and see what time it is."

Nan (a little Negro girl) obeyed the order and returned with a grin; she said:

"Missus, de big hand ob de clock is up, and the little one am crossways."

"Plague take you, you little blackskin. I have a great mind to pull your ears. For the life of me I can not learn that little Negress anything."

"Curse them; I have found them to be more *trouble* than *profit*. To gratify you I will come in a few moments. I have something rich to tell you."

The Widow laughed, and at the same time she stroked back her jet-black hair, showing a set of teeth white as pearls.

"Nan!"

"Yes, Missus."

"Go and tell Bill to put Queen in the barn, and feed her well."

Nan shot away like an arrow and returned in a few minutes.

"Missus; can't find him."

"Where did you look for him?"

"In de orchard, Missus."

"I do not know what to think of that little wretch; she knows as well as I do that Bill is chopping wood in the bottom. Go, this moment, down to the bottom, and tell Bill to come here immediately, you little simpleton."

Nan went off at a snail's gait.

"You, Nan?"

"Marm?"

"If you don't hasten, I'll skin you when you return."

"Yes, Missus."

In a few moments Bill, the servant man, came up and said:

"I declar; here am Massa Ben," and gave vent to one of those hearty laughs the African is so noted for. One would have supposed that his whole frame would have fallen to pieces before he closed his mouth.

"Take Queen, Bill, to the barn, and feed her well," said the Widow. "Do walk out on the piazza, Mr. B. It is much pleasanter; be seated; will you take a glass of wine, cider or ice-water?"

"Thank you, I'll take a glass of water."

"Go, Nan, and get a tumbler of ice-water."

Nan returned, holding the glass in her hand.

"How dare you bring water in your little black hand to a gentleman?"

"'Deed, Missus, I could not find a tray."

"Where did you look for it?"

"In the wardrobe, Missus."

"Do hear that little imp!"

Mr. B. at the same time shaking his sides, laughing at Nan and her mistress.

"Be off you little idiot."

The Widow and Mr. B. then drew their chairs up side by side.

"Do tell me, Mr. B., the news of the village. Is Sally Jenkins married?"

"I think not."

"No! I am rather inclined to think she is too fickle-minded. You know Josh Barnes is dead in love with her, and, indeed, he is a clever fellow. I am inclined to think he is too good for her."

"You know women are strange beings, and few can account for their choice, taste and notions."

"You are quite complimentary; thank you kindly. (Mr. B. laughed). If I did not know you so well, I would take you to task," said the Widow with a happy smile on her countenance. "You have rather a strange idea of women."

"Not by any means; I am their friend. I have received but little gratitude in return. I advocated your cause to-day."

"Pray explain to me in what way, Mr. B.?"

"Frank Clifton [L. Jacobs], at the village, is desperately in love with you."

"Ha, Ha!" ejaculated the Widow, her face flushed as she gave vent to her feelings.

"I told him that you were worthy of any gentleman's esteem, and hoped that he would succeed. Like most men; I suppose he feels a delicacy in urging claims of matrimony."

While they were conversing, a neighboring woman, Mrs. H., living near by, thinking that Mr. B. remained longer than usual, made an excuse, went to the house, and asked for the loan of a book.

The Widow entered the sitting room, returned and presented Mrs. H. with the desired book.

"I am always pleased to accommodate my neighbors, but Mrs. H. invariably makes it a business to come to my house when I have company. She is, indeed, an inquisitive and a talkative woman. I have not been in her house since the death of my husband. If she was capable of taking a hint, she would not come here. Excuse me for interrupting your conversation; do give me the history of this gentleman who has become smitten with me. Is he handsome, accomplished, and of good origin? You know I wish no other as a suitor, nor would I wed with a man that did not possess these qualities."

"You are hard to please."

"That is just my sentiments; I am ready whenever I meet a gentleman whom I know possesses those qualifications, and believe that he will fulfill the duties of a companion."

"Perhaps you will not meet with so good an opportunity soon," said Mr. B. "As to qualifications, he is an excellent business man, and has an education suitable for his position. He is strictly honest and reliable. I am satisfied in my own mind that he is worthy to accept the heart and hand of any accomplished lady."

The Widow shrugged her plump, round shoulders, and remarked with a smile:

"That will do, as far as it goes. You know my dear husband was a gentleman by birth and education. How much do you suppose him to be worth?"

"It is said that he is worth thirty or forty thousand dollars."

"That would be a handsome little fortune for one who is not extravagant or wasteful?"

"I should think it would."

"Do bring him down; I have a curiosity to see him."

The remark caused Mr. B. to smile.

"I promised him an introduction to you; I thought it advisable to ascertain whether it would be agreeable to you."

"If he is good-looking, perhaps chance may favor him. You know that I am a woman possessing a noble and generous heart. I have been raised tenderly and kindly, and to marry a man that was not truly my equal would render me unhappy for life."

"I am aware, madam, that you are deserving a worthy companion. I have no desire to select a choice for you. I merely delivered my message and expressed my opinion. Mr. Jacobs is the gentleman."

"Thank you, I have heard of the gentleman, and from reports I would suppose that the fair sex have no charm for him, and that he was a stranger to the sensation of love, having neither taste nor desire for the association of ladies."

"There is a time in the history of men's lives that radical changes occur, old ideas decay and new ones take their place. I once read of a nobleman who never entered the society of ladies. He shunned them on all occasions; the door of his affections seemed to have been forever closed against them. While strolling out for a morning's walk, he accidentally met a peasant girl returning from market. She had sold her little produce and was homeward bound. He inquired her name and residence, and in three weeks from that date she was his happy bride. What do you think of that?"

"I suppose Love has no eyes, is deaf to criticism, and blind to the smiles and frowns of the world."

"She made him a happy companion, though plucked from Nature's garden—a raw flower. With the hand of affection, he planted it in richer soil; she grew wise and twined around his affections like the vine round the towering oak. The storms nor the ills of life marred not their happiness; their bark sailed calmly upon the ocean of time as they drifted on to the great ocean of eternity."

"The evening is far advanced; I must be off, hoping that you may be able soon to decide for yourself."

"Your company is so agreeable I regret much your leaving."

Bill had Queen at the door in readiness. She was as restless as a leaf in the Summer's breeze; she stood pawing the ground and champing her bit, eager to bound like a deer to her coltish home.

Mr. B. mounted.

"Kiss Nellie and the babes for me," said the Widow. "Good-bye, good-bye."

Queen leaped off like a hare and soon neared the old farm on which she was raised. As she came in sight of her mates grazing in the meadow, she neighed. Peter, Mr. B.'s hostler, caught the sound, and hastened to open the gate.

"How do you do, Peter? How are you getting along?"

"How do, Massa? I is well and am glad to see you, sar."

"How is your Missus, Peter?"

"She is well, sar, but in bad humor."

"What is the matter with her, Peter?"

"Don no, sar; dat boy ob Missus H., dat libes on the road above de Widow's, been here, sar, wid a note."

"Can it be possible that wretched woman has written an untruthful letter to my wife?"

Leaving his sable groom, he started for the house. The dog, seeing his master, gave him a welcome bark; this brought little Maggie and Willie to the door. They cried at the top of their voices: "Ma, here comes pa." They gave a leap and each was in his arms; he kissed them with a father's love. He thought strange of his wife not coming to greet him.

"Where is your ma, Willie?"

"In the bedroom, pa; she's been kying, pa."

He entered the hall, Sue, the housemaid, got a glimpse of him.

"'Fore the Lord, dar's Massa Ben," cried Sue.

"How have you been, Sue?" said Mr. B.

"Tank you, Massa, I is well."

"How is your mistress?"

Sue glanced her eyes toward the bedroom, shook her head and whispered in his ear:

"Trouble here, Massa; sure as I is born."

Mr. B.'s countenance in an instant looked depressed. He hastened to the chamber-door and rushed in.

"How do you do, dear Nellie?"

"I have no further use for you, sir," said Mrs. B. "Your presence is disgusting in my sight. How foolish have I been to love a wretch like you. I had rather be an inmate of the alms-house than to live under *your* roof. Release me from this prison; I have loved you with a woman's pure love. You, sir, have blasted and withered my earthly hopes."

"What possesses you, Nellie? What notion has entered your brain?"

"I, sir, have in my possession a note of your conduct, written to me by a woman of truth and veracity—of your conduct at the Widow's. You, sir, have been there since noon to-day. Your actions there were unbecoming a gentleman. Three weeks to-day you have been absent, and to think you came within a mile of home and remained there all day."

The fires of jealousy long smothered was kindled on the altar of her heart.

"You are the last woman that should accuse me thus, and one that has long been your confidential friend," said Mr. B. "Had I known that you entertained the slightest suspicion of my fidelity and the Widow's chastity, I never would have entered her door."

"I am satisfied, sir," said Mrs. B., "that you are as guilty of misconduct as Arnold was of treason; you deserve a felon's fate. I left a home of comfort, ease and happiness, to become bone of your bone, flesh of your flesh. See your gratitude? What justifiable excuse can you offer—what evidence can you produce—to exonerate you from a charge so unjustifiable and unbecoming the dignity of a gentleman. None, sir."

"You speak as one whose reason is dethroned."

"Better that you hide your guilty face than to attempt to enter a plea of innocence. Your actions for the last six months have been suspicious to me. You had more business at the village during the six months past than for three years prior. Your excuse was that you were compelled to attend the 'Lodge.' An excellent excuse, indeed, to shield you from suspicion."

"Nellie, have you got through?" said Mr. B. "I am mortified at your actions, you accuse me of that which I am not guilty of. The Widow is as pure as a new-born babe. She loves you with a sister's love. How could you listen to that wicked woman's lies. The Widow told me, when she came for the loan of a book, it was only an excuse to excite you, and to create mischief. She envies you, your happiness and the society of your friends. Her object is to destroy your peace, and to blast those cherished hopes you have so long nourished. Have you yet to learn that women are envious and jealous of each other's success, and would condescend to use the most artful intrigues to accomplish their wicked designs. I am the same man in principle, honor and sincerity to-day as I was when I led you to the bridal altar. Time, nor the varied changes of business matters, have not caused my love to grow languid or cold towards you. You are the idol of my heart. Mrs. H. alone is responsible for your unhappiness. I am truly sorry to think that you are so credulous as to give countenance to her reports. My kindness to the Widow has been of pure friendship; knowing that she was a lone woman, thrown upon the world without an earthly prop to lean upon, her bosom companion taken from her and consigned to the narrow limits of the grave. I felt towards her as you once did; deeply interested in her welfare. I supposed then you were free from the passion of jealousy."

"You, sir, appear to be a good judge of 'human nature.' You seem to understand the dispositions of women to a charm, and their imperfections. Men, with you, are all angels! Your explanations have not removed my suspicions, nor established a proof of your innocence. Do you remember, sir, the first Sabbath in last month at the village church? The Widow accompanied us by your invitation. I was convinced from that very hour of your guilt. During the service at the chapel, I perceived that you were becoming attached to her. Your mind was not the least interested in the excellent discourse delivered by the pastor on that occasion. You seated yourself on the upper side of the Widow instead of taking your seat between us; and, for the life of you, you could not keep your eyes off her; she was your only attraction. I was not the only one that noticed your actions on that occasion. And still you profess to love me! Such love is mockery; your pretension of love to me is hypocritical. You cannot induce me to believe any such stuff. I am no child to be fed on pap. You, sir, are as deep as the sea. Thanks to Mrs. H., I have got on your track; I shall trace you to your den. I shall leave no stone unturned until I fully establish your guilt or innocence; an outrage against woman's honor to be thus treated and sacrificed. Men are worse than Satan desired them to be. What woman unincumbered with man would listen to their flattery or allow herself to be drawn into their net—knowing what I do of the torments! None would leave a home, however humble, to become the drudge and slave of man. Life has no charms for me. No, none. If it were not for those dear babes I would take a leap into eternity, and bury my sorrows and cares in the silent tomb. Speak not to me."

Mr. B. turned away, with tears rolling down his cheeks, and a heart burdened with sorrow.

Mrs. B. called to Sue, her Negress servant:

"Sue, go immediately and tell Peter to come to my room."

"Yes, Missus." Before Sue left she exclaimed: "For de Lord sake. Missus, what am de trouble wid you an Massa Ben? I declar, Missus, I is like one in de troubled sea. I had vissions, night after night, and I have prayed to de Lord to show dem to me, so I could know dem. I hab wept dis day like a weeping willow, Missus; I did want to come into de room to see you; I see you so full ob trouble I did want to talk wid you. I as been in de same trouble, Missus. I declar to de Lord, if I didn't want to be dead and in de grave. I prayed to my blessed Lord night and day to take de trouble away, and gib me the victory over my enemies; de Lord did answer my feeble prayers, and my troubles went like a short Summer's day. Hab fate in de Lord, Missus; He will make de crooked way straight, and the hilly, lebel. I know dese men bar watching. For de Lord sake don't tell Massa Ben I say anyting; I spect dis trouble long time. Dat Widow is more cunning as de serpent; I believe Massa Ben loves her."

"What makes you think so," said Mrs. B. "Have you seen any familiarity between them?"

"Well, Missus, one day I pass de parlor door I see Massa Ben sitting on de sofa close by de side ob de Widow. He get up just as I look in de door, de Widow look at me, den at Massa Ben; I see mischief in her eye."

"Where was I, Sue, when this happened?"

"You had gone up to de orchard, Missus."

"Why did you not tell me, Sue, about it?"

"Well, Missus, de Lord say, 'Blessed am the peace-makers;' dats de reason, Missus; I tought it best to say noting."

"It is very strange, Sue, that you kept it from me."

"Missus, de Lord said: 'De sins of de vicked shall find dem out;

Bress de Lord it has come true. I know it, and prayed for de Lord to show you dese tings, dat you might see dem wid your eyes. See how good de Lord am; He am de same God dat delivered Daniel out off de lion's den. Trust in Him, Missus, and He deliber you out of dis trouble; bress His holy name."

"Do you think so, Sue?"

"Yes, Missus. If I had de wings ob a dove, I would by in de kingdom dis hour. Den dis poor body and soul be ebber free from sins, sorrow and death."

"Sue, would you leave me in this hour of my affliction. You talk about heaven as though you had been there. Death is a terror, Sue, to the purest of earth's saints: Don't talk so silly about matters so serious. I promised myself to make Mrs. H. a visit and ascertain the facts relative to this affair."

"Dat am de place to go, Missus; I be bound dat you find out dar all Massa Ben's tricks; I lub you both as my own dear children; dat woman will tell you de hole truth; my poor heart bleeds for you; I tink Massa Ben act so bad."

"Go and tell Peter to saddle Bet; I have delayed it much longer than I intended."

Sue delivered the message, and in a few minutes Bet was at the door. Mrs. B. leaped upon her back, and said:

"Sue, take good care of the children in my absence."

"Yes, Missus."

"Good-bye, Sue!"

"De Lord bress you."

"I had like to forget. If your Master should return in my absence, you need not tell him where I have gone."

"No, Missus, nebber; I is too smart for dat."

Bet seemed honored to assist her Mistress on her mission; she was as playful as a cat and as innocent as a lamb. She was not long in bringing her Mistress to the gate of Mrs. H.'s residence. Mrs. H., seeing Mrs. B., hastened to open the gate, and exclaimed:

"Dear me! how do you do? I am delighted to see you; I have news that may be of interest to you. Do alight and walk in; or, would you prefer sitting under our old favorite oak?"

"I prefer being seated here, as it is much cooler," said Mrs. B.

"I'll bring you a chair; make your pony fast to the fence; or, shall I take her to the barn?"

"She is gentle as a kitten."

"Indeed, she looks cunning; I would like much to own her. What a splendid head and form! She reminds me so much of a favorite pony my husband bought me a year ago. Unfortunately he died. Will you allow me to take your hat and shawl?"

"Thank you."

"I am so pleased to see you! Can you not remain over evening?"

"I should be pleased to do so, if it was in my power; you know that I have two little children, and they compel me to be home at night."

"Is it not strange to see the unhappiness in families resulting from the imprudence of women and the depravity of men?"

"Indeed it is; that is my mission here to-day."

"I assure you I feel interested in your behalf, knowing that you have been treated shamefully. I scarcely know what to think of such conduct. I would leave a man who would treat me as your husband has treated you before the setting of the sun; I would drop him like a hot-iron. It ought to be me instead of you; I would make him know the strength of the law. I saw your husband ride up to the Widow's about noon to-day; his horse was put in the barn, and he remained there until dusk, knowing at the same time that he had been absent from you for three weeks. I thought it rather a strange proceeding; I made it my business to go over to the house and ask the loan of a book, for an excuse to satisfy myself. They were seated together, as loving as two doves. As I turned the corner, I took them by surprise; they seemed confused. The Widow arose from her chair, and looked as silly as a child. Of course I did not let on to her that I noticed their embarrassment; I simply asked for the book; your husband sat speechless, and for the life of him he could not look me in the face. Are not women silly creatures to allow themselves to be made the dupes of men?"

"I have long esteemed the Widow as a lady worthy of my confidence," said Mrs. B.; "but it is well said that 'human nature is frail.' She is the last one that I thought would be guilty of destroying my happiness. For several months past I felt inclined to think something was wrong. My husband has seemed indifferent to me, and has not treated me as kindly as in former days. At the same time I thought perhaps business matters caused him to act thus."

"I know of him making her handsome presents. Did he ever tell you?"

"Yes; he told me that he gave her a shawl. I thought nothing of it; she showed it to me; I regarded it as pure friendship."

"I don't think that is all he gave her; I saw her have a splendid parasol that could not have cost less than twenty-five dollars. You are aware that she never visits me, or I might have ascertained the price of it. I am unaware of the reason why she don't visit me; I suppose she is stuck up like many others, and thinks herself better than anyone else. To tell the truth, I have had my opinion of *her* for a long time; she is a snake in the grass; I would not trust her with a husband of mine out of my sight. Kate Henderson's troubles were similar to your own. Her husband gallanted Mary Sheppard to the last party at the village, and left her at home to slave; she came over and asked me my opinion; I knew that he thought more of Mary S. than he did of his wife, Kate. I have seen Henderson and Mary evening after evening, walking out, while his wife was drudging at home. Finally, he treated her so bad that she asked me what she had better do; I told her the sooner she got rid of him the better it would be for her; he had scarcely the second shirt to his back. Jack Blue would marry her to-morrow if she would obtain a bill, and advance her money to fee her counsellor. This he told me out of his own mouth. She is the biggest dunce of a woman I ever knew of; she says she cannot give him up. Poor simpleton! Did you ever hear of such nonsense? She partly agreed to marry Blue at one time, provided she could obtain a bill. He gave her several handsome presents to my knowledge. He is, indeed, a model of perfection, and would make her a happy companion. She is industrious as an ant and as nice a little housekeeper as you will find anywhere. I truly sympathize with her; you know that she fears outside talk; that is all folly for a woman to allow herself to be imposed upon. Mr. Blue is a man of means and would give her anything in the world if she would obtain a bill and accept his offer of marriage. He fell in love with her at a party given Mrs. Dalton last fall. Since then they have been the best of friends. I suppose you are acquainted with Martha Lovejoy?"

"Slightly; I have seen her at several parties given in the neighborhood. She is a fine looking woman. Is she married?"

"She was, but by my assistance she obtained a bill. William

Lovejoy was a good provider for her; but for her life she could not love him."

"That seems to be a strange course to pursue; I should think that a woman would be competent of knowing whether she loved a man or not before she married him."

"The match was made by her parents, much against her will," said Mrs. H. "You know it is hard for a woman to be really happy under such circumstances. She is to be married in two months from to-day."

"Pray, to who?"

"To Henry Lockwood."

"Indeed; how long have they been acquainted?"

"He was her first beau, and [she] was engaged to him before she married Mr. Lovejoy. At that time they were both young and foolish, they fell out about some trifles, as young people often do, without any real cause. Old coals, you know, will kindle."

"Do you think he will make her a good companion?"

"I do; he is a gentleman in every sense of the term; he is intelligent and has an amiable disposition; at the same time she is resolute and determined. Many of her friends advised her not to leave Lovejoy; she consulted me; I gave her my opinion; in a few words I told her, 'If you are not happy, seek you own happiness.' She is a woman of strong mind; she has courage and the grit. When her case was tried she had much to contend against. Public opinion was against her to a great degree; I stuck to her, and so did Lockwood; he is well deserving of her, for he worked faithfully to free her from William Lovejoy. She loved Lockwood, and regretted much that she had not married him instead of Lovejoy. I am an advocate of 'Women's Rights;' and if I see them imposed upon, like a faithful sentinel, I invariably give warning. You, perhaps, thought it bold in me for addressing you that note?"

"Not so," said Mrs. B. "I am under many obligations to you for the interest you have manifested in my behalf."

"You see I have a splendid view from my door, and can see every one that visits the Widow's house; I have been watching them a long time."

"They were sitting like two lovers?"

"Yes; and your husband looked as sheepish as a wolf. He never so much as looked up. They were excited and confused, which induced me to telegraph to you."

"Thank you kindly."

"I would not have missed it for the world; is the Widow on good terms with you?"

"She is!"

"What a wretched woman she must be; she is as full of deception as an egg is of meat."

"What do you think is the best course for me to pursue?"

"There is but one effectual remedy. Domestic troubles are like an aching tooth. The only hope I see to secure you from future difficulties and unhappiness is to obtain a bill; I have been divorced three times, and would demand it again to-morrow if necessary. I never will condescend to lick the hand that smites me, nor love a man who does not respect me."

Mrs. B. smiled and said: "Did you not find it difficult in obtaining so many bills?"

"No; I never applied twice in the same State. I invariably made it a rule, wherever my lot fell, to procure the influence of the most influential gentlemen of the county, and never failed to succeed in gaining their confidence and assistance. It is true, I was rather good-looking, which may have produced an effect," and she laughed heartily.

"If you succeeded on the merits of your good looks, I will stand a slim show."

"Ho! ho! ho! I never have seen the day that I was as good-looking as you are now."

"Thank you for your compliment."

"Not at all. You know men are just silly enough to assist any good-looking woman; many of them will spend their last dime if a woman but smiles at them. A woman that is as good-looking as yourself is never without admirers."

"Thank you; what do you think it would cost me for counsel fees?"

"Dear me, ask Col. M. He is an excellent counsellor; he is a great admirer of the society of ladies. I know of his having obtained several bills for ladies; he would not accept a dime from them for his services."

"He is very generous; I would like very much to make his acquaintance."

"He left just three weeks to-day for Warrenton Springs; his health being poor I think it's likely he will remain there during the season."

"I have become so thoroughly disgusted with Ben that I hate him."

"I know the intense hatred of a woman when she turns against a man who has wronged her."

"If I really thought that I could obtain a bill, I would apply at the next Term of Court."

"In my mind there is not the slightest doubt that you will succeed. Whenever I take a dislike to a man, I never cease to agitate the matter. I keep the pot aboiling; I am a good fireman, and make things terrible hot for them when necessity requires it. In one of my difficulties with my second husband, I entertained such a disgust for him that I was really meaner to him than I should have been; I found that without war I could not gain my freedom. I finally excited him to such a pitch that he slapped me. That was just what I wanted in order to secure a bill. A woman can do more hurt with her tongue than a man can with his physical strength. It will not be amiss to relate some few facts touching the case; I am satisfied that I can drum up several more witnesses outside of myself. That Widow is a wolf in sheep's clothing, and well deserves to be made an example of. Do you suppose that she is aware that you are on her track?"

"Not that I know of; I am confident she does not."

"Did you stop as you came up?"

"I did not."

"She'll think it strange of you passing without stopping. I think it will be to your interest to keep on good terms with her until we get our plans all arranged."

"I detest the sight of her."

"I have learned to stoop to conquer my enemies, and never fail to come out victorious. My advice to you is to call on her when you return, and act as though nothing had happened. It will afford us a better field to operate in, and we may glean more reliable information by working cautiously. Are you acquainted with Polly Hopkins?"

"I am not."

"She is one of the best workers in matters of this kind that I know of."

"Is she reliable?"

"She is the most confidential old creature I ever met with; she is the best fortune-teller in the State; we had her employed in Martha Lovejoy's case. Had it not been for her, I think we would have been defeated. Martha had the poorest excuse of a lawyer to defend her I ever saw; it would take a clap of thunder to arouse his intellect—if he had any—and a broad-ax to sharpen his ideas. A pettifogger is the worst curse a community ever was afflicted with, and the poorest specimen of humanity."

"And, pray, who was her counsel?"

"G. B. Bowers."

"He is a stranger here, is he not?"

"He has been here the last six months; he is from Alexandria, where he practiced until driven out by hunger; I was told he never gained a single case during his practice there. He is a perfect wind-bag and makes great pretensions until he gets his fees; you then have to be continually urging him up. In my opinion, he is better adapted for a servant; we would have lost the case had we relied upon his judgment and abilities; through my advice, Martha employed Judge S."

"Is he a good lawyer?"

"He is one of the best in the State; he is an able counsellor and adviser. The only objection that I have to him is, he appears to be slow and tedious; I judge this from his conversation. Most men speak three words to his one."

Mrs. B. smiled and said:

"Perhaps he believes in the teachings of the Bible: 'Think twice before you speak once.'"

"Ha! ha! ha! you are something of a theologian. He never flatters his clients; he is candid and frank, which adds greatly to his success."

"What do you think of Peter Logan?"

"My opinion of him is, he would not only sell his clients, but rob the dead. Did you know Alfred Kraft?"

"I have heard of him."

"He lived thirty-five miles from Fairfax Court House, on what is called the 'Old Road.' Logan was his counsel for many years; he was taken down suddenly with the intermittent fever; for a few days his case appeared hopeful; finally, he got worse and gave up all hopes of recovering, as did his friends; he appointed Logan as his administrator. No security was demanded of him for the faithful discharge of his duty. Kraft had implicit confidence in Logan. Mr. Kraft's wife died one year to the very day he was buried. They left four little children, the oldest not over nine years of age. Logan robbed those poor little orphans of every dollar, and is now living in ease and luxury, while those little ones are provided for by kind friends. That is his history."

"He surely must be a miserable wretch. Ah! how can he die in peace guilty of a crime so heinous and black?"

"It is true. Old Squire Givens and him are said to be partners, guilty or not guilty. If you are brought before old Givens' Court, he will fine you as sure as you stand before him; a fine and costs is his rule of justice. He applies it in all cases if possible. He has hoarded up riches, by fleecing the poor. But, thank God, there is a higher Court at whose bar the world shall be judged, the king and the peasant are equals there!"

"I must be going," said Mrs. B.

The sun was now gliding down behind the Western hills and tinged the peaks of the lofty mountains with its golden rays as it passed away.

"When shall I expect you again?"

"In two weeks."

"Aunt Polly will be on hand to-day two weeks. If we start in after the Widow we will make things warm for her."

"Does Aunt Polly know me?" asked Mrs. B.

"I think not," answered Mrs. H. "She has been residing in Alexandria most of her time; she lived on Union street, No. 48."

"Oh! I have heard of her notoriety; I must really go, as it is getting late."

"I will lead your pony up."

"Thank you; I have taught her to wait upon herself."

She called Bet, at the same time holding out her hand. Bet came up and licked her mistress' hand like a poodle.

"What a knowing creature she is! She looks as cunning as a little child," exclaimed Mrs. H.

"I have taken great pains to educate her; she is very intelligent and has a lamb-like disposition. The babies can go under her; she will step over them as carefully as a person."

She mounted.

"I hope your next visit will be agreeable and profitable."

"I hope so."

"Do stop at the Widow's as you pass."

"For your gratification I will do so."

"I had rather you would use policy."

"Good-bye, good-bye."

"Now, whatever you do," continued Mrs. H., "accept of no compromises; ask no questions and give none. Be a woman. Let us show to the lords of creation that we intend to defend 'our rights' to the last; and, remember, agitate. We will make a good case of it. If luck attends us, we will bring you out 'right side up with care.'"

Mrs. B. left. Bet speeded off in an easy gallop, and soon halted at the Widow's gate.

The Widow seeing her, exclaimed:

"Why, Nellie, is that you? Where have you been?"

"Up the road on business," replied Mrs. B.

"You mean thing; did you pass my house without stopping?"

"I was somewhat in a hurry."

"Tell me how [your] children and your husband are?"

"Thank you; they are well."

"Dear me; how I would like to see those little darlings. Do get down, Nellie, and kiss me; you are the meanest thing that I ever saw. I would not think of passing your house more than I would to fly; without calling. Do come in, Nellie; I have something new to tell you."

"I will stop a few moments."

As she alighted, the Widow embraced, kissed her, and gave her a playful slap.

"I have a great mind to give you a good whipping, you naughty thing."

"What have you new to tell me?" asked Mrs. B.

"Mr. B. has caught me a new beau. What do think of that?"

"Who can it be?"

"L. Jacobs."

"You don't tell me so? Is is possible?"

"Nellie, do tell me what you think of him?"

"He is a gentleman highly respected. I know girls that would give the world to get him."

"Nellie, don't you think him old-maidish? I have heard of him, but have not had the pleasure of seeing him to my knowledge; I know nothing of his disposition."

"Men of his style and character are a scarce commodity in this market; you had better strike the iron while it is hot!"

The Widow shook her sides and roared with laughter.

"Do you really think so, Nellie?"

"I do."

"Nellie, I know you are a good judge of human nature; if you really think so, I'll set my cap for him."

"Do so; I must really be off."

"If you will go, kiss me good-bye, and be sure to kiss the babies for me and give my love to Mr. B."

Mrs. B. mounted, and Bet was not long in making the port of destination. Peter was on the look-out; he hastened to open the gate. "How do you do, Peter?" Bet darted through the gate like an arrow. Sue ran out to meet her mistress.

"Sue, I suppose you thought I had forsaken you?"

"No, Missus. Neber fear dat while dem babies here. I habe been looking for you dis long time."

"How are my little darlings?"

"Dey is fine; I gibe dem a cup ob mick, and put dem to bed."

During the conversation Peter, the hostler, came up, and took charge of Bet.

"Peter, feed her well; I know she must be hungry."

"Yes, Missus," replied Peter, and started for the barn.

"Sue, have you heard anything since I have been absent?"

"No, Missus; eberyting has been as still as de grabe. Jack Hubbard been here to-day; he says Massa Ben be home to-night or to-morrow. Missus, do tell me how you find tings up dare?"

"Ah Sue, I am not surprised; matters are just as I supposed them to be. I am now decided; I shall not stand such conduct much longer; I intend to apply for a bill of divorce."

"Wat am de bill ob diborce?"

"A bill of divorce, Sue, means separation of man and wife by a legal process of law."

"Den, Missus, you'll no more be Massa Ben's wife?"

"No Sue; I wish to the Lord I had never seen him."

"Well, Missus, what am to become ob me and dese little childrens?"

"I will see that you are provided for; you have long been my faithful servant, and I will reward you for your constancy and devotion to me. I feel very tired and must lay down; make me a cup of strong tea, Sue, and bring it to my bedroom."

"Missus, will you hab some toast wid it?"

"A small piece of dry toast, Sue; prepare me in the morning a nice broiled chicken and some milk biscuit for breakfast."

"Yes, Missus."

When morning came, Sue had breakfast prepared in good style, and knocked at the bedroom door to arouse her mistress. No response came; she knocked a second and a third time without effect, and said: "I wonder if poor Missus am dead?" She then tried the door and found it secure; she rushed out and called:

"Peter, come here; I believe Missus am dead!"

He laughed and said:

"Wat for you tink dat?"

"I been knock, knock, knock, at de bedroom door; Missus no answer."

"Ho! ho! Missus ben up dis two hours; gone take a walk down in de meddow."

The morning was one that would have enchanted the soul of any lover of Nature; the air was pure, balmy, and fragrant with the odors of flowers dripping with the dew-drops and nodding to the gentle breezes of heaven; the sun was just peeping from behind the Eastern hills; all aided to make the scenery lovely, and the music of the birds floated on every wafting breeze.

In a short time Mrs. B. returned to breakfast. Sue was busy in arranging her cooking utensils. Mrs. B. stole silently up behind her, and seized Sue in a playful manner. Sue was frightened and came very near leaping into the fire.

"Missus, am dat you? You scare me almost to death; I been knock, knock, at your door and nobody answer; I tought you dead; Peter tell me you go take a warke."

"No danger, Sue, of my dying, I trust, until I make an example of my good friends."

"Dat am so; hee! hee! Missus; I tell you dis bressed morning dat de debbil am bout dis place."

"Yes, Sue."

"I set up in de kitchen de oder night Missus; I hear someting out in de yard like people's talking; I go out dere; I look eberywere; I see noting; I come in and fastend de door; I sit down by de fire; de door fly open; tree peoples walk in; de one in front all dressed in white, de odder two in black; my hair stand on my head; I trimble; to sabe my life I could not move; dem in black wanted to come up to me; de one in white stand before dem, and said, 'De time is not come! we must depart!' Oh! Missus, I fell on my knees and prayed to de Lord to take dem away; de door slam and bang like de earthquake; de house rock like de cradle; when dey went out, I got up and went to shut de door; someting pushed de door open and said: 'It's time you had left here; what are you doing here dis hour of de night?' I tought I die, Missus; I nebber be so scared in my life; de sweat rolled down me like water been poured on me; I left de kitchen and started for de bed; I's so weak I tought I'd fall on de floor."

"Sue, you are so superstitious; it's nothing in the world but imagination."

"Well, Missus, if dat am magination, I nebber want to see it again; I tell you, Missus, dis place am haunted; I lay one night wid my eyes open'd; I felt de cobber mobe; I pull it up; something pull it away; I pulled it again; something jerked it on de floor; I look; I see noting; I get up out ob de bed to pick up de cobber; someting open de door; I drop'd de cobber and got under de bed; a light shined in de room like a lamp, and den all was dark; I tought I'd sink."

"Why did you not speak of this before, Sue?"

"Well, Missus, I thought you might get 'fraid, and lebe de house."

"Nonsense; Sue, you talk so silly."

"Dat am as true as I born to die, Missus."

"Sue, I have no desire to hear any such foolishness; I suppose you were dreaming."

"No, Missus; I see it wid dese eyes open."

During the conversation, Peter entered the bedroom with a letter for his Mistress, who opened and glanced over it; she exclaimed, "I am betrayed."

"Where did you get this letter, Peter?"

"Mr. Shepherd, de post-office man, gibe it to me."

"Peter tell me the truth; have you not been to the Widow's?"

"No, Missus."

"For the life of me I cannot place confidence in you; what questions were asked you when this letter was given to you?"

"Nofing, Missus."

"Peter, don't tell me an untruth."

"Well, Missus, he asked me if dar was some trouble wid you and de Widow."

"What did you tell him, Sir?"

"Don no, Sar."

"Ah! Peter, you are a deceptive Negro, and well deserve to be punished. As sure as your master returns you will not fail to give him a full history of what has transpired during his absence; it is your style; I guarantee that my so-called companion has related this matter to the Widow."

WIDOW'S LETTER TO MRS. B.

Main Road, July 15th.

Mrs. Brown—Much to my mortification and surprise I have been informed that you and others are in league to vilify and traduce my character without the slightest justification. From our long acquaintance and the friendly relations we have sustained to each other, *this* alone should have induced you to act justly and honorably toward me. Why did you not speak of this like a frank woman yesterday, when you were here? No! You concealed your hatred. How could you be so treacherous and deceptive? I am truly proud I have no remorse of conscience. I have lived above suspicion, and I have never given *you* the slightest cause to treat me so unbecoming a lady. A pure heart fosters not the poisonous reptile of revenge. Frankness is a virtue and conceals not deception. You have acted unwisely and imprudent; unbecoming a woman of your standing and education. I consider those who condescend to stoop so low far beneath my notice. Duty alone prompts me to speak in my own defence, bring my accusers *face* to *face* and I will silence them, like Maria Antoniette; her persecutors led her as a lamb to the slaughter; sacrificed her upon the altar of hate; a purer woman the sun never shone upon. Am I the victim of a base conspiracy, selected to be sacrificed upon the bloody altar of revenge? Do I merit it? No! I demand a fair and honorable investigation. Remember that *virtue* is a jewel, a character ungalvanized is of far more value than gold and silver. How true the friendship of earth is but a name; it has become merchandise; sold in the market-place to the highest bidder. How could you be so unfeeling and unjust to *one* who has ever been your true and faithful friend? There is a day coming when the secrets of all hearts will be revealed. The pure *and the just* shall receive justice at the hands of that *Judge* who shall judge the world at his righteous bar. "There the wicked shall cease from troubling and the weary shall ever be at rest."

Widow.

Sue, with astonishment, gazed at her mistress while scanning over this letter, and said:

"Missus, am dat letter from de Widow?"

"Yes, Sue, it is; and I will bet my head your master has posted her."

"She am de angel of Satan; she ought to have her back broken, dat Widow; dat Peter, Missus, who bring dat letter, he am deep as de sea, and de truf he nebber tell; he am a chip of de old block; I know his father Jack; he was de biggest liar in de world; and all dem darkys he raised is bad; how can him, Peter, be good? You send him to de post office, I belibe he been to de widow's house, and tell her all about dis ting."

"What makes you think so, Sue?"

"Cause de oder day wen we talk, he put his head in de door and drew it back for fear you see him."

"Like his Master, Sue; Peter is mean enough to do anything. But we should give Satan his due; I don't think he was at the Widow's."

Little Maggie, during the conversation, fell off the porch and screamed; this attracted their attention to the front door, and greatly to their surprise they saw Mr. B. riding down the lane leading to the barn. Sue exclaimed: "Missus, dar am Massa Ben." He rode up to the barn and called Peter.

"I declar, Massa, I'se been looking for you dis three days."

"Peter, take good care of Queen."

"Yes, sar." Peter led Queen to the barn and his master followed.

"Well, Peter, how are matters here? How is your mistress and the children?"

"De childrens is fine, sar; Missus am de same."

"Is she still in bad humor?"

"Yes, sar; and for the Lord sake don't tell her I tell you, Massa; she rode me up Salt Ribber."

"What for, Peter?"

"I get a letter from de post-office man, sar, and gib it to her. She seem very mad, sar—for de heaven sake don't breve what I tell you."

"What did she say, Peter?"

"She says she hab no faith in me, sar; dat I am your pet Nigger. She tell me not to tell you about dat letter, sar. Now, Massa Ben, don't say I tell dis ting."

"Who do you think it's from, Peter?"

"Well, sar, I speck it's from dat Widow who hab made all dis fuss."

"Did she say it was from the Widow?"

"No, sar; but you see dat Sue am very cunning; she's Missus' friend, sar; I heard dem talk about de letter; I listen at de door, sar; Sue, she started to see if I was dar; I run to keep dem from seeing me, Massa."

Mr. B. hung his head and started for the house; as he entered the house Mrs. B. met him. He said:

"How do you do, Nellie?"

"How dare you speak to me? If I was a man, and a woman would treat me with the contempt I have treated you, I would shun her as I would a viper; you lack the dignity of a *man* and the principles of a *gentleman*. Consider me, sir, forever your enemy. You have planted revenge and hate deep in my heart. Your doom, sir, is forever sealed."

"Nellie?"

"Begone from my sight; the look of you disgusts me. You, sir, are past atoning for your sins."

"Nellie, do you intend to destroy my happiness, and bring me to the grave in sorrow? I have possessed the patience of Job; I still entertain for you a husband's love. Time can never blot you from my memory, though you have treated me harsh and wrongfully."

"I, sir, scorn your *love* and detest your sympathy for myself and those cherished babes. If I thought for a moment that they possessed a single trait of the man who is their father, I would bind them fast with the cords of death and with joy close their eyes forever upon the scenes of this world of wretchedness, notwithstanding they are the apples of my eye and the jewels of my heart. You have doomed me forever to sorrow and affliction. I feel like one that has no earthly hope; far better would it have been for me had I never hearkened to the treacherous deception of man. Death, truly, would be a welcome messenger to me; I would welcome his stern decree."

"Nellie, oh! that I could induce you no longer to be the slave of jealousy and suspicion; free yourself from that tyrant, it knows no bounds; it has no sympathy; with its crimson hand it has slain thousands of victims. I trust you will see your error and repent; walk in the highways uninhabited by suspicious characters. Then it is you will be happy in time and eternity. Would the wise and the good be the victims of jealousy, hate and revenge? No! no! never! Jealousy discriminates not between its friends and its foes. Ever give me a heart pure from the curse; clothe yourself with those noble principles that make woman the beauty of creation. If you will but hearken to those instructions, the sunshine of peace will again dawn upon your pathway; the present and the future will again be joyous to you. Be wise and cease forever to be the dupe of jealousy."

"You have admonished me to walk in the highways uninhabited by suspicious characters. Do you practice the doctrines you teach? No, sir; far from it. I command you to return to the paths of virtue and chastity, and walk in the ways of the just. Cease to do evil and learn to do good. No longer be the cringing fawn of sin and vice. Be a freeman! Stand upon the broad principles of right. But, alas! I fear it is too late. Vice has become your companion and sin your guide. Who, sir, informed the Widow of our troubles? Who advised her to be on her guard? You, sir, have become her lackey; you have condescended to drag your domestic affairs before the world and painted in glowing colors your deception. I'll make known and publish your crimes and prove you are the evil genius I have represented you to be. No hypocritical garb shall conceal your sins from the eyes of the world; you have given it publicity; I'll follow the example. Truth is as terrible to such as the roaring peal of distant thunder is to the untrained colt. Will you be admonished to repent of your sins? Take refuge under the wing of a merciful God. You, sir, are competent to draw beautiful illustrations from fiction, and would have the world believe that you are as pure and innocent as an angel. You have played well your part, but at a fearful cost. The way of the transgressor truly is hard; 'thy sins have found thee out.' Are you the man to reprove me? No! cleanse your heart and your hands from all unrighteousness. Time has told the doleful tale; thrice guilty are you. Your heart is like a sepulchre, it is full of rottenness and corruption. You advise me to clothe myself with those principles that make woman the loveliest of creation. Go, thou Judas, and clothe thyself with the garments of purity and dignity."

Reader, we shall leave Mr. and Mrs. B. for the present and return to Mrs. H. and her friend.

CHAPTER II

"Lawrence, do you intend going to the village?" asked Mrs. H.

"Yes," said Lawrence; "I shall start soon."

"Call on Aunt Polly Williams and ask her to come down; I want to see her on particular business."

"What in the world do you want with the old humbug of a fortune-teller?"

"Don't talk so simple. Will you do as I have requested? It is a little out of your way, and if you deliver the message she will be here inside of an hour. It is but a short distance to her place from the road."

"Yes; I will tell her; at the same time I want but little to do with her kind."

Lawrence delivered his message. The old soothsayer started and in a short time she knocked at the door of Mrs. H.'s dwelling. The door was opened by the landlady, who said:

"Dear me, Aunt Polly, I am delighted to see you; I have a good job for you, and if you arrange your plans right you can make money out of it."

"Yes; that is just what I am after," said Aunt Polly. "I am the woman to secure it if opportunity permits; tell me who the parties are, and if you think they will stand bleeding."

"Mrs. B. and her husband are at dagger points all about this neighbor of mine, the Widow. She has caused Mr. B. to neglect his wife and children; he is much devoted to the Widow. I put Mrs. B. on his track; you know that I am a good hand to catch such fellows. Mrs. B. wants to gather sufficient evidence in order to obtain a bill; she is to be here to-morrow; I recommended you to her very highly; she wishes to secure your services in this affair; she has the means; if not, a friend (unknown to her), has offered to assist her if required; this gentleman is desperately in love with her, but she knows it not; indeed we are very fortunate to get lovers for our clients."

"I will play my part to perfection; you can rely on that," replied Aunt Polly. "What do you think she will really stand to get this matter under her control. We can operate more successfully for her than any other parties."

"She has implicit confidence in me; I have been the main spring in opening up the affair; I informed her of the pretended friendship of the Widow and the faithlessness of her companion; I caught him nicely; I am satisfied to get this whole matter in a nutshell; I think she will give one hundred dollars; at the same time if she flinches, do not refuse fifty."

"I will propose to her one hundred dollars, and you must express your surprise at the reasonableness of the charge, individually, for fear that she might think we were equally interested in making it a speculation. When do you expect her, to-morrow?"

"Yes; everything will be in readiness; I think it will be a capital idea to bring Martha Lovejoy over with you; you are aware that she has been in the same fix and is an excellent talker."

"That is a good proposition, and I think it will have its effect," said Aunt Polly. "I am a little in a hurry; I cannot stay long. So good-bye."

"Don't fail to be on hand to-morrow at the appointed time," remarked Mrs. H.

Mrs. B., according to promise, made the necessary preparations to revisit Mrs. H. the following day. She started the next day, and, to avoid passing the Widow's, she concluded to walk. She ordered Sue to take good care of the children; bade Sue good-bye, and started across the lower meadow. Strange emotions filled her throbbing breast; half an hour's walk brought her to the door of Mrs. H. She knocked and was received cordially.

"Kiss me, darling," exclaimed Mrs. H. "I am delighted to see you; you look like one heartbroken. How have you been getting along since you were here?"

"The storm still rages," replied Mrs. B.

"I expected it, and have been thinking of you ever since you left. Walk into the sitting-room. (They entered). Mrs. B., allow me to introduce you to my lady friends, Mrs. Martha Lovejoy and Mrs. Hopkins," who were anxiously waiting her arrival.

They received the introduction very cheerfully, and seemed highly gratified. Mrs. B. looked at Aunt Polly with surprise; she looked more like a visitor from the Land of Pandemonium than a human being.

"I suppose, Mrs. Hopkins, that you are aware of my mission here to-day?" asked Mrs. B.

"You look like one in great distress of mind," said Aunt Polly. "I have no doubt that you are the subject of sorrow and disconsolation."

"It is just this: I wish to know if I am wronged by my companion and the woman who professes to be my devoted friend. I wish you to tell me who the parties are that seek my destruction, and designate them definitely; I also wish to know your price."

"Well, dear child, you know it requires a deal of time, energy and shrewdness to get this matter in shape; I shall charge you one hundred dollars."

"That is more than I can afford," replied Mrs. B.

"This is a delicate matter and should be handled with kid gloves," added Mrs. H., with a bright smile on her countenance. She then remarked to Mrs. B. that she had news of interest to relate to her.

"I suppose those present are cognizant of it?" asked Mrs. B.

"Yes; we are confidants. I should apologize to you for being so inconsiderate or hasty, as you may think. However, I have a duty to perform. There is a friend of mine and well-wisher of yours, and I do not hesitate in saying that he loves you—but for the world he would not have it made public; he is an intimate acquaintance of your husband; he is desirous to advance your interests in this matter, and will give any amount to assist you in your difficulties."

Mrs. B.'s face flushed, and anger seemed to have taken possession of her soul; she asked:

"Are not these strange proceedings? Who do you take me to be? I came not here to seek lovers, but friends, and in search of simple justice."

"I hope, dear Madam, that I have not offended you. Regard me as your friend, and not your foe. I know that the sentiments you have expressed are just and right. At the same time friends are often necessary to enable us to succeed in accomplishing our desires in life."

"I am truly aware of that; friendship is one thing and love is another. When you speak of love, that produces a horror in my bosom; I ask not for the love of any man. If I have a friend who will render me assistance, without obligating myself to him, it would be accepted, but I must first know that he is a gentleman of principle. Who is the gentleman?"

"He is, indeed, a gentleman of the first class; and, if you should succeed in obtaining a bill, and would accept his offer, you would never be in want of a dollar nor the comforts of life, the longest day you live. Is it not so, Martha?"

"Yes, indeed! I almost begrudge her the chance to become the wife of such a splendid man; he is a perfect gentleman; I have known him for the last four years. There are girls in this neighborhood who would give their two eyes to get him; I don't know but what I would try to shuffle off my old man if I thought I could induce him to make me the offer, notwithstanding I have no fault to find with my companion—he treats me like a baby. At the same time, you know, money is what induces us to love."

"Ladies, I have heard patiently your advice, and thank you kindly for the interest you have manifested in my behalf," said Mrs. B. "To offer me a friend who is, perhaps, an entire stranger into my confidence and affections, and relate to him my private affairs is more than I can condescend to do, however honestly disposed he may be. What would my friends think of me for pursuing such a course? Would they not forsake me? Yes, and leave me a total wreck. I should feel more than condemned to act thus imprudent; I love my children with a mother's love; I have a character to sustain, and trust I may never bring disgrace upon myself and children. Do inform me who this gentleman is, and what has induced him to make me those liberal propositions? I think it not only a bold act, but indeed a rash one."

"J. Oldham is the man," replied Mrs. H.

"Can it be true? I never could be more surprised; he is the last man that I would have dreamed of," exclaimed Mrs. B.

"It is nothing to have a gentleman friend in these times, and it is becoming fashionable."

"It is very strange that he should again fall in love with me."

"Then he is not a stranger to you?"

"No; he is not. He is the first man that I ever loved in days gone by, when my heart knew no sorrows, no anguish, no pain. But I am truly surprised to know, after the lapse of so many years, that he loves me still; I cannot realize it to be true. I have known him since I was a school-girl. We have often played together in the morn of life."

"Allow me to inform you that I have a confidential letter from him for you, which I will hand you to read," said Mrs. H. She drew the letter from her pocket and presented it to Mrs. B., who glanced over it, and strange to say, tears, which had not flown since the death of a beloved brother, stole down her cheeks; she struggled to conceal her feelings, but in vain. She said:

"Can it be true?"

The letter read thus:—

Centreville, Aug. 2d.

Mrs. Brown:

Dear Madam—I hope you will pardon my boldness, and perhaps (in your judgment) imprudent course. The esteem I have long entertained for you, alone induced me to address you this letter—hoping you will not condemn me for the liberty I have taken in writing you these lines. We are all creatures of circumstances, and few there are who have not erred in life. I know you to be a lady of high mental culture and refined feelings. You have long been in my thoughts by day and dreams by night. But I will not dwell upon the past. I am satisfied you merit far better treatment and a more congenial companion. Duty prompts me to offer you aid, and my influence; I feel deeply interested in your behalf, having known you from childhood. Then you were as cheerful as a lark in autumn.

Time has not obliterated you from my memory, though our acquaintance has not been renewed for many years. How true, the world is the great theatre and the sons and daughters of man the actors. Life has its joys and its woes, and but few of us are free from sorrow, and the ills that attend the journey of life. It is the love of God that sweetens our sorrows and enables us to bid defiance to life's transitory and bitter trials. What man possessed of a soul or a spark of dignity could treat you so? I am not deceived in the man who claims you for his wife. He is unworthy of so noble a woman, and is far from being your equal socially or in point of education. Remember I am still your friend, and hesitate not to make known to me your wants. Hope is truly the anchor of the soul, and enables many to keep their heads above the surging billows of despair. I trust that a brighter future awaits you. The true test of friends is to be judged by their acts. Give me a friend who is ready and willing to rescue me from the whirlpool of adversity, and the wheel of misfortune, under which so many have been crushed. Too oft we have the pretended smiles of some who hesitate not to obstruct our pathway. I fear not an open foe; deliver me from foes in disguise; they are dangerous. My purse is open to you. In conclusion, I have faith in your integrity, and have thrown myself entirely upon your mercy; I wish you to destroy this letter. Carry this matter to the grave—a secret. I shall be more than happy to advance your interests, socially and pecuniarily.

Yours affectionately,
Joe. Oldham.

Mrs. B., after glancing over the above letter, seemed to be shocked as by electricity. In a few moments she exclaimed:

"Who would have believed it? Love, truly, is like a stream; ever running on, and on, to the great ocean of affection. Its course is hard to change."

Mrs. H. smiled, Martha Lovejoy laughed heartily and said:

"Love is a giant to contend against. He takes his subjects captive at his will and binds them as with chains."

"What do you think of things now?" inquired Mrs. H.

"I dare not say," she replied with a faint smile upon her countenance.

Aunt Polly raised up her spectacles and remarked:

"It's time our work had commenced."

"I consider the price very exorbitant, as I said before," said Mrs. B.

"I refer you to Martha Lovejoy; she was in the same fix as yourself; she is present and can speak for herself."

"I am indeed indebted to you, Aunt Polly and Mrs. H., for my success in obtaining a bill," said Martha. "Had it not been for your influence I would still be the slave of my former husband. Had I not been young and foolish ne'er would I have been caught in such a trap. It's true, we are all liable to be deceived. That marriage was the great error of my life."

"We often choose those for our bosom friends whom nature nor heaven never designed," continued Mrs. H.

"Truly," said Mrs. B., "no mortal has experienced it more sensibly than myself; I am miserable; brought on by the frailty and deception of the man whom I have been so silly and foolish as to love and cherish; I would give the world to be released from him; I have fully made up my mind to die rather than to live with him. I would suffer myself to be banished to some distant isle in the sea, uninhabited by the children of men."

"I truly sympathize with you," said Aunt Polly. "It is a horrible condition to be in."

"I will give you fifty dollars; twenty-five I will pay you in hand, the remainder I'll pay at some future time."

"I will accept your offer on one condition."

"Pray what is the condition?"

"I have no desire to choose for you a friend and a lover; it is for your benefit alone I speak of him, knowing that you can find no truer friend in all Virginia. Remember well he is no short stock; no bob-tail aristocracy; he is of the first families of this country, and strictly a gentleman. No woman in your condition should for a moment hesitate to accept the offer."

"I have every reason to believe he is all you represent him to be. I have known him many years and once loved him as my own life. Time has blunted that love. You must remember those things cannot be consummated in a day. It behooves me to act prudent and cautious. One step in the wrong direction would, perhaps, blast my success forever."

"That is true, child; but ventures make merchants. Without some risk, there is little to be gained."

"Indeed, if I were in your situation I would take such chances every day in the week, and care but little as to what outsiders would say," said Martha Lovejoy. "I have never known it to fail; a woman who demands her rights, secures ten friends to one enemy. You know in such cases, right or wrong, women have the sympathy. It will never do for you to cringe or yield to public opinion. We are so constituted we can live down whatever may come against us if we aim to do so. You must remember that society will not clothe nor feed us. For instance, look at Mrs. Woodland. She moved in the first society; she was the idol of the rich, surrounded with every comfort that one could wish to enjoy. She applied and obtained a bill, and in six days after she married George Appleton. The news spread like wild-fire; her name was on every tongue; but, like a match, it soon died out. She had the grit, although not justified in leaving Woodland."

"Dear me," said Mrs. H., "I am astonished, Mrs. B., you certainly cannot realize the position you are placed in. It is an old saying, and a true one, that drowning men will catch at straws, but you seem determined not to seize the bark floating upon the sea of life, which has come to your rescue; you are blind to your own interest; a woman who has been treated wrongly, and abused. It is indeed folly for you to let this offer pass. It is not uncommon in this country for a woman to be engaged to another before they obtain a bill. I tell you, you must prepare yourself for every emergency, and stop your ears to what babblers may say. Make up your mind, thoroughly, to seek your own happiness, regardless of the praise or condemnation of others. Martha Lovejoy, like yourself, hesitated; I urged her up and on, until she became as fearless as a lion. Take courage and be a woman after my own heart; go forward and you shall come out victorious. Make up your mind; decide to-day; you may have a thousand offers, but never one like Oldham's. No! never! Your disposition and his would match to a charm."

"Ladies," said Mrs B., "I claim to be a woman having some judgment and experience. It is a true saying, 'chickens should not be counted before they are hatched.' If I was free to act, I would be better able to decide. To commit myself would subject me to ridicule and slander. Secrets, you know, are very hard to keep, and especially where the parties are not equally interested. We do not always know our friends from our enemies; we often have friends in disguise. Many have been sold at the hands of those they regarded their bosom friends. And it is common for parties equally guilty, to turn State's evidence. Secrets are difficult for women to keep; a person cannot be too cautious. Were I to accept Mr. Oldham's proposition, my husband has his friends and hirelings stationed on every highway, and [at] every social gathering in the neighborhood; and should the matter leak out, it would be a powerful weapon in the hands of my enemies; and if defeated, would leave a stain upon my character that could not be erased. Nature is frail at best. I have no desire to fall a sacrifice at the hands of my enemies. You must admit the risk is an adventurous one."

"Mrs. B., we should not become alarmed of danger when there is none," urged Aunt Polly. "If you will here agree to correspond with Mr. Oldham, I will accept your offer. This is the proposition I offer to you. I accept the twenty-five dollars, which is no money for a job of this kind."

"It would be easy for me to answer his letter, but other considerations are to be looked at in the mean time."

"Ho! ho! That is a matter strictly between yourselves," added Mrs. H.

Aunt Polly requested the ladies to take their seats around the table. She then drew a greasy pack of cards from her pocket and drew down her spectacles, remarking, "These never lie to me." She cut them and held them for Mrs. B. to draw, which she did with a trembling hand, and laid them cautiously upon the table. Aunt Polly turned them face upwards and laid them in a row. With an excited laugh, she exclaimed, "We have got them! We have got them!" Martha Lovejoy clapped her hands and said, "I knew it, I knew it!"

"That's so!" cried Mrs. H.

"Madam," said Aunt Polly, "you can see for yourself; here is your husband and the Widow, side by side; here is the house, located, according to those outside cards, on the main line, which denotes the main road, that runs directly past her dwelling; you see the window and the shed-porch that covers the front; and here is the hall running directly through the house. In it you see the wretched man and woman holding a consultation; this is your renegade husband, and this (pointing to a card), is your pretended friend, the Widow."

"I am fully satisfied of their guilt, now," replied Mrs. B.

"Nothing could be plainer. If you continue to live with Brown you deserve to be discarded by society," said Mrs. H.

"I hope, Madam, that you are now fully convinced that Aunt Polly is no humbug?" exclaimed Martha Lovejoy.

"I would not live with such a man; he will never, never, mend his ways," said Aunt Polly. "I have only to say, in conclusion, take the counsel of a friend, and accept the offer made you by Mr. Oldham."

"It is a matter that requires consideration," said Mrs. B.

"You seem determined to be doubtful of success," said Mrs. H.

"Your case is as clear as the noon-day sun. A woman never had a better case to carry into court; all depends entirely upon an able counsellor."

"I should dislike very much to obligate myself without being confident of fulfilling my pledge. I prefer not to accept any favor from Mr. Oldham at present. At the same time I feel truly grateful to him; his kindness I shall not forget."

She paid Aunt Polly twenty-five dollars in hand, and said:

"Ladies, the day is far advanced and I must hurry home."

"Be careful and not commit yourself on your arrival home," said Mrs. H. "We must teach men that they cannot destroy a woman's happiness and restore it when they think proper to blarney, or, as they call it, to humor us. If we expect to retain the respect due our sex, we must teach them an impressive lesson. Let them know 'our rights' are sacred, and that our feelings are not to be tampered with. He who violates the marriage vows should be branded with the mark of Cain on his forehead. Allow not public sentiment to deter you from the right. Pay no attention to it. You now have it in your power to release yourself from the tyrant; and, if you don't do it, it is your own fault. Martha Lovejoy married in three weeks from the day she was divorced, and is to-day the happiest woman in this section of the country. Is it not so, Martha?"

"It is, indeed," said Martha. "You should embrace this opportunity. I would make an example of the Widow and him. I would dissect them as a physician would a corpse; I would teach them the fearful consequences of deception and guilt; indeed, I would wool her head for her; she deserves to be skinned alive."

"You can depend on it," said Mrs. B, "that I will do my duty to bring them to justice. Good-bye, good-bye (they all kissed her). When shall we meet again? I shall endeavor to have an interview with you before the trial."

"I should be most happy to hear how you are getting along," said Mrs. H.

"We have accomplished much to-day," said Aunt Polly.

Mrs. B. laughed.

Mrs. H. remarked after Mrs. B. had left:

"Did you notice her countenance? I am satisfied we made a favorable impression upon her mind in favor of Mr. Oldham."

"She is Oldham's property," said Martha; "there is no doubt of it. Did you notice her when you handed her the letter?"

"Indeed I did."

"And, pray, what a change," added Aunt Polly. "We worked her up beautifully."

"You know that she felt embarrassed under the circumstances, and seriously objected to the proposition; we advocated Oldham's claims like Philadelphia lawyers, and made her present condition deplorable in the extreme; we did it to a charm," said Mrs. H.

Aunt Polly laughed and said:

"You are the best attorney in the State. You never fail to convict a prisoner, guilty or innocent, and clear your client."

Mrs. H. smiled and said:

"I consider it a compliment."

"You are deserving it, and indeed I should hate much to have you after me."

"Ha! ha!" ejaculated Mrs. H. "Knowing you as well as I do, I would let up on you to a degree, if you were the prisoner and I were employed to prosecute you."

"I would not trust you," replied Martha.

"We have secured her," said Mrs. H. "They seldom outwit me, you can rely on that; I will make Oldham pay for it. I never work without compensation."

"Do you think she will muster courage to leave Brown?" asked Aunt Polly. "I am inclined to believe she loves him still."

"If she continues to live with him it will be because she is defeated in the bill. I painted things to her in livid colors; and indeed, made things appear twice as bad as they were. I hate the Widow anyway; I think but little of the Widow and Mrs. B.'s husband; they put on considerable airs with me at Josh Brown's; we were invited there to dinner; they treated me very coolly and thought me beneath their notice, and unworthy of their society; I am determined to get even with them."

"I have long thought the Widow stuck up," said Martha. "I have been to several parties where she was, and had to receive a new introduction to her each time; we have now got the drop on her, and we will put her through a course of sprouts before we are done."

"She is nothing but an upstart," said Aunt Polly. "I knew her long before her husband died; he was as fine a man as ever walked in shoe-leather; she led him a dog's life, and rendered him unhappy. She was continually flirting around with Tom, Dick and Harry. She knows me as well as either of you; we have past and repast, but she never spoke to me in her life. When we get the thumb-screws on her, we'll make her know who we are, and bring her down to a button-hole lower; she'll not carry such a high head."

"The beauty of it is," said Aunt Polly, "we have not only got her under our control, but we are bound to make money out of the affair. Mrs. B. readily consented to pay fifty dollars, and I am satisfied that Oldham, when he hears of the progress we have made in his behalf, will not hesitate to give us a hundred dollars to commence with; he loves Mrs. B. as dearly as a baby loves milk. Love has no price. We will make him pay."

"Money is what we are after. When do you expect him?" inquired Aunt Polly.

"I look for him to-morrow," said Mrs. H. "I shall give him to understand it requires money to carry this affair through, and without it little can be accomplished."

"He will not hesitate to pay any price you may ask him," said Martha. He is liberal and has the means. Do you think she will answer his letter?"

"I wish I was as sure of getting a thousand dollars as I am that she will answer it," said Mrs. H. "At the same time, I give her credit for not committing herself to us."

Readers, we must here leave Aunt Polly, Mrs. H. and Martha for the present, and return to Mrs. B. She seemed highly gratified with her visit. She returned and entered her once happy home. Sue and the children welcomed her. She embraced and kissed the children and shook hands with Sue.

"Missus," said Sue, "I almost gibe you up. Do tell me how tings is? I want to know so bad."

"Ah! Sue, things are in a deplorable condition. You have no idea, nor a mind capable of comprehending the magnitude of the wrongs I have been subjected to; your Master Ben is a wretched man. Has he asked for me during my absence?"

"Yes, Missus, he did; I tell him don no; he say he suppose you gone on some foolish errand."

"Where is he, Sue?"

"I speck he is at de barn talkin wid dat Peter. He and Massa Ben hab been talkin ever since he come from Wash. Jackson's; and dat Peter tell him ebery ting he knows."

"I am aware of that, Sue; I never entertained a favorable opinion of him from the first time I saw him. I know that he leans with his Master."

During the conversation, Mr. B. walked in and remarked:

"How do you do, Nellie?"

"Speak not to me; I have lost all respect for you; I know enough of you to hate you in your grave, from what I have learned this day," replied Mrs. B.

"Nellie, do you mean to torment me unto death?"

"Yes; and after death if I could. You are a dissembler, a knave and a villain; I have solved the problem of your crime, and am prepared, at any time, to prove your guilt. Your deeds of darkness I shall not be long in bringing to light. You are devoid of dignity and have violated a right I hold as sacred as my life; your soul is blackened with crime, sin and vice. You have desecrated every principle of right. Satan has a bill of sale of your wicked soul. My fond hopes, cherished love and blissful anticipations are withered forever. My heart is made wicked. Oh! that I could offer to God a prayer in your behalf that would be acceptable for your sins. It is too late; forever too late. Those who stand upon the everlasting principles of eternal justice are immovable; the storms of persecution, and the whirlwinds of slander shall harm them not; 'they shall walk thro' the Valley of the Shadow of Death, and fear no evil'; 'but the guilty fleeth when none pursueth.'"

"Nellie, you have become a maniac; you are insane; from whom have you gleaned your information? You speak as one who was educated in the school of superstition and misplaced confidence—these principles with you are predominant; your reason is dethroned; bring forward those evil geniuses; I will confront a regiment of them, and prove every assertion to be as false as Lucifer. You are the subject of witchcraft; you are treading in the path leading to perdition. If you continue you are ruined; every hope of happiness is gone; those individuals are the mothers of falsehoods, and like Satan they go about seeking whom they may devour! They are the disciples of sedition, malice, hate and contempt. You have not hesitated, Madam, in wounding your devoted female companion, a wound deep and sore, made with the weapon of slander and reproach. A wound I fear you can never heal. Your advisers are leading you to shame, degradation and disgrace. Be wise and prudent. I stand innocent. I defy the world to convict me. You are determined to agitate this matter until your name will be heralded from city to city, and from village to village; your character will become food for the vultures of society; you are deaf to truth and blind to reason. I possess every virtue that characterizes manhood, dignity and morality; with these weapons I am prepared to engage the foe. I entertain no fears. 'Truth crushed to earth will rise again!' Justice is doomed never to die. Mark you, Madam, from this hour I have no compromises to offer. If you intend applying for a bill—the sooner the better. I will there meet you and my accusers face to face; I shall shake their castles and fabrications to atoms. Thousands of innocent victims have been tortured upon the rack of slander. I fear not its horrors. They have thrashed me thoroughly with the rod of persecution. My heart is made to bleed at every pore; they cannot drive me to despair, nor will I ask for protection or shelter under the emblems of compromise. No, never! I have long been silent. Your plans of stratagem are too thinly covered to be concealed. I am sorry to say that I have become satisfied that 'all is not gold that glitters!' I have admonished you to hearken to the voice of reason, and to be guided by truth and love."

"I have listened to you, sir," said Mrs. B. "You never fail to make an able defence; like Aram who was tried before a British Court for his life, you are competent to plead your own innocence. I shall believe it only when it is proven; Aram pled for his life; his eloquence held the court spellbound, tears stood in almost every eye, yet he failed to establish his innocence; he died a felon's death for the crime he had committed. I have positively decided to apply for a bill at all hazards at the next setting of the court. There is no further use in discussing this matter; you have brought it upon yourself; I shall likewise sue for the custody of the children and my third of the property."

"It is not uncommon for married women to become infatuated with lovers on the outside," replied Mr. B.

"I desire you to explain yourself; I will not allow you nor any one else to question my chastity without producing facts to bear them out. You are the first, and should be the last, to insinuate anything against my character, sir. Take care that I don't make you eat your words. As low as you are in the scale of degradation, I supposed you to be more manly. What do you know of me, sir? I defy you to bring aught against me; I am a lady in the strictest sense of the term."

"Do not women err? I am sorry to say they are blind to their own faults. When a woman becomes dissatisfied with her companion, she will pick any flaw or use any pretence to justify her in leaving him; I have humored you like a spoiled child."

"I wish to hear no more from you. I know enough of men to hate them the longest day I live. Do you think, sir, I would ever become the dupe of another man? You have taught me a lesson—one that will certainly last me to the grave. To think you have accused me of loving another man! Is it not strange that this has just entered your imagination? None but a corrupt and malignant heart like yours would harbor such thoughts without the slightest provocation. Well, well," she said, with a shrug of her shoulders and a toss of her head.

"I have not been delicate in expressing what I believe to be true. Time may change or confirm my belief. I shall live, however, let the results be what they may. I admit such things try the souls of men, and sink many forever in the gulf of despair, never to rise again. I rely solely upon the justice of that God who reads the secrets of all hearts."

"Oh! yes! You have become very pious. It is a great pity that you did not think of Him ere this. If so, you would be happy instead of miserable. You will see that your Widow will be made an example of in this community. Satan desires no better disciples than you and that false-hearted woman. I trust that the God of heaven may have compassion on your soul. I wish to have nothing more to say to you, sir, on the subject."

Mr. B. had in his possession the letter that Mrs. H. presented to Mrs. B. from Mr. Oldham, but she knew it not.

We shall now leave Mr. and Mrs. B. for the present and return to Mrs. H. and Mr. Oldham.

CHAPTER III

According to promise Mr. Oldham called upon Mrs. H. He knocked at the door. Mrs. H. hastened to open it.

"Dear me, Joe, is that you? I am pleased to see you."

He was soon seated in a plain but neat sitting-room.

"I expect Martha here every moment. I suppose you would like to know how we succeeded during our first meeting with reference to you? We accomplished a great deal in a short time; she was really the hardest subject that I ever met with—in reference to your proposition. Otherwise, things worked to a charm; I am satisfied that she felt embarrassed and disliked to commit herself to us who were almost entire strangers to her. When I spoke of you, I saw there was a change in her countenance. I conversed with her uninterruptedly for full three hours. You know that I season things high; I made her believe that she was the worst treated woman in Virginia; I pled nobly in your behalf, and pointed her to a future fraught with happiness, joy and peace, if she would only consent to become your bosom companion."

"How did she seem to take it?"

"To tell you the truth, Joe, she was completely speechless for some time; she struggled hard to conceal her feelings. To one unacquainted with human nature, she might have deceived them in that particular; but I am too old, and have been too long in the business. The fountain of love, long chilled by the cold winds of life, gushed up warm in her soul when I spoke of you. I have not the slightest doubt that you will have the game. Not that she told me so; I judge it from her appearance."

"Do you think that she really loves me?" asked Mr. Oldham.

"Yes, dearly. The consummation of the entire affair is only a question of time."

"Has she made arrangements to secure a bill?"

"Bless you; we have been arranging plans so as to enable her to succeed."

During the conversation Martha stepped in.

"How do you do, Martha?" said Mrs. H.

She bowed very politely; Martha returned the compliment; Mrs. H. further said:

"Do be seated, Martha. We have a deal of work to accomplish yet; I suppose that you are aware that I drafted Aunt Polly to aid me in the work? Martha also volunteered to assist us. I do not claim the victory so far won, for both of them were equally interested in the work, and they are the parties to be employed in an enterprise of this kind. They are also close observers, and are not slow in carrying any weak points that may be presented; they are good planners and sharp trappers."

"What are their charges for services rendered in this matter?"

"Aunt Polly, you know, gains her livelihood by taking such jobs; I told her that she should be well rewarded. Mrs. B. gave Aunt Polly twenty-five dollars in hand, which is only a drop in the bucket towards accomplishing the work before us. Here is Martha; of course I expect to compensate her."

"Indeed, Mr. Oldham," said Martha, "you may think yourself one of the lucky ones. We have put a beautiful feather in your cap." She spoke with the ease and grace of a countess."

Mr. Oldham smiled and replied:

"Thank you, kindly; I feel greatly indebted to you, ladies."

"Mrs. B. is a charming woman," continued Martha. "She has every qualification to make a worthy companion; she is generous, kind and loving."

"Do you really believe that I can win her affections?" asked Mr. Oldham.

"Ask me if the wind ever blows, or if the sea ever runs dry," rejoined Martha.

Mr. Oldham laughed heartily and said:

"I judge by that, that you are sure of my success."

"I am, sir; I am satisfied that she loves you dearly. I would not be surprised to hear that she had already written to you."

Mr. Oldham laughed and drew the letter from his pocket.

"We never fail to succeed. What did I tell you?" said Mrs. H. to Martha. "Mr. Oldham, have faith and much will be accomplished."

Mr. Oldham here read the letter from Mrs. B.:

Brown's Farm, August 3d.

Dear Mr. Oldham—I am happy to inform you that I received your kind and welcome letter through the kindness of your esteemed friend, Mrs. H. I feel under ten thousand obligations to you for your generous offer, and the interest you have manifested in my behalf. I am pleased to know that I still have a place in your affections. Notwithstanding that years have intervened, you have not blotted me from your memory. You say that you love me as of yore. I must acknowledge that your unexpected letter has made a lasting impression upon my mind. You feared that your offer to assist me would be rejected and your letter to me made public. I assure you it is so full of love, friendship and sympathy, no one possessing a spark of humanity could discard it. I hesitate not in saying I have long been the subject of cruel and harsh treatment. I have ever been a kind and dutiful wife to Brown. I am compelled to make the bold attempt to free myself from the deceiver. I may receive public censure; but, after all, I alone am to be the judge of my happiness, and not others. I have borne with him until nature revolted and patience rebelled. My love for him has turned to hate, and every feeling of kindness is obliterated by his wicked deeds and acts to me. I cannot think of living longer with such a monster. No! never! I would rather be the wife of the humblest peasant on earth, if I knew him to be just, honorable and upright. What is ease, wealth, or affluence, without peace and confidence? A palace to me, indeed, would be a prison, if happiness did not dwell there. I have been sacrificed by the man I loved. Oh! how frail is human nature, and how liable to err at any unguarded moment. He has fallen deep in the whirlpool of vice and crime. What has been his gratitude to me? Deception, hypocrisy and guilt. I regret much the course I am compelled to pursue. When I think of my dear babes, it brings tears to my eyes, and fills my heart with grief. But am I the only one that has been forced to take shelter under the wings of love, extended to them by others, whose hearts are warm and generous? No, we are so singularly constituted, that women cannot be happy without an object to love. I have long felt as if I had no earthly friend, nor hope of future bliss. In your letters to me, give me still further encouragement to bear up under my affliction and sorrows, and may I still look forward to the day of sunshine and happiness which I trust will burst through the sombre clouds of despair. My affections are chilled. "Now is the Winter of my discontent," when all should be joy and peace. I shall be happy to correspond with you from time to time. We must be cautious; I am already accused of loving another. And however pure and friendly your correspondence may be, if made public, would be injurious to both. Your friend, Mrs. H., is a true woman, and I never shall forget her kindness.

Yours, sincerely,
Nellie Brown.

P.S.—Write soon.

Every word that fell from his lips, as he read the letter, seemed to be food for their craving appetite.

"Well! well!" exclaimed Mrs. H., "I can scarcely believe it is from Mrs. B. Perhaps some one is trying to steal a march on us."

"I am sure it is from her," said Martha. "Let me see the handwriting."

Oldham presented her the letter.

"I have seen the hand-writing, and am satisfied it is hers."

"Don't you think we have accomplished wonders?" asked Mrs. H.

"You deserve great credit, and have been far more successful than I anticipated," replied Mr. Oldham.

"I thank you for the compliment," said Mrs. H. smiling.

"We are trumps and are fully competent to open a school," added Martha, laughing.

"I am sure we are competent to teach. We would get many pupils," said Mrs. H. "Few understand human nature so thoroughly as to arrange matters of this kind successfully. Domestic teaching is much needed, as there is a deal of dissatisfaction among married folks. It is a science not easily acquired."

"Few appreciate its worth," Martha continued. "Human nature is hard to fathom. Mr. Oldham, what does the Widow think of things about this time?"

"Did you not hear that she wrote Mrs. B. a stinging letter?" said Mrs. H. "For the soul of me I cannot imagine who posted her. Mrs. B. said she was satisfied that her husband had acquainted her of the fact. Mr. Oldham, I am not deceived in the man."

"He will wish that he never had been born; far better would it have been for him that a millstone was tied around his neck and that he should be cast into the deep," said Martha.

"When he reads his fearful doom, as if written with the finger of the living God, he will tremble and seek shelter. He is a wretch undone," said Mrs. H.

"I would like to be his 'jack-catch;' I would crack his neck as I would a pipe-stem. He is unworthy to live and unfit to die," said Mr. Oldham.

He then asked the question:

"Do you think it advisable for me to keep up the correspondence with Mrs. B.?"

"I do," said Mrs. H. "You now have matters in your own hands; and if you don't control them, it will be your own fault. It is an old saying, and a true one, 'Procrastination is the thief of time.'"

"You deserve to be complimented for your labors," said Mr. Oldham. "I will give you an order on Mr. Peterson, the merchant at Centreville, for four hundred dollars. Retain one hundred for your own services and present Mrs. B. with the remainder."

The following is a copy of the order:

Warrington Turnpike, Aug. 23d.

Mr. Peterson: Sir—Please pay to the bearer the sum of four hundred dollars, and charge the same to my account,

Joe. Oldham.

Mrs. H. thanked him kindly and said:

"This is more than I expected to receive at this stage of the proceedings. However, you shall not be disappointed in our undertaking. So far, things have worked beautiful."

"That is all right," said Mr. Oldham. "I leave matters entirely in your charge. I trust Mrs. B. will not delay in having the papers filed for a bill; and if she is defeated, I am a ruined man; my entire hopes are centred upon her."

"I am sure she will apply at the October Term of Court, and before Christmas Day she will be yours," said Martha.

"You will then consider yourself one of the happiest men in the State of Virginia. You will not only be her bosom companion; but you will also have to assume the responsibility of a father. She has two children, and I have not the slightest doubt they will be assigned to her by the Court," said Mrs. H.

"It would afford me great pleasure to become their tutor and provider. I am partially fond of children," said Mr. Oldham.

"No man need be ashamed of them, they are well behaved and have excellent manners; I would give the world if they were mine. Mr. B. will struggle hard to retain them. He loves them dearly; at the same time I think him incompetent to raise them properly."

"He is a man of no refinement, having but a meagre education at best; he has been more successful in business than most men of his stamp," said Mr. Oldham.

"You know it is said, 'a fool for luck,'" remarked Mrs. H., with a laugh.

"What do you think Mr. B. is really worth?"

"I should judge him now to be worth twenty thousand dollars," replied Mr. Oldham.

"Indeed; I have heard of late that he has made rather reckless speculations. If he is worth that amount, Mrs. B. will have a handsome little sum. They cannot keep her out of her third, if she gets justice," said Mrs. H.

"She will get every dollar of it, if she employs a good counsellor—one that cannot be bribed," said Martha.

"I know pettifoggers in this State, that would rob the grave of a deceased friend," said Mrs. H.

Reader, we must now leave Mrs. H. for the present, and again return to Mrs. B.

"Sue?"

"Mum?"

"Go and tell Peter I want him immediately."

Sue obeyed and Peter shortly after entered his mistress' sitting room.

"Peter, I wish you to take this letter to Fairfax and deliver it to

Lawyer Higgins. Saddle a horse and don't delay a moment. Be home, if possible, by to-morrow night."

She gave him a few dollars to defray his expenses, and ordered him to secure an answer. Peter started on his mission.

"Missus, 'pose Master meet Peter, and ask him where he am gwine? You know dat de cross-road come into de turnpike five miles dis side of de old meetin' house, and Massa Ben may come dat road."

"No, Sue; your Master will not. He has gone the upper road to Warrington and will remain there at least four days, as he has business to attend to."

"Den it is all right; I do trust you will be free from dis trouble and come out as shining as de sun. Hab faith in de Lord, and he will bring you through."

"I intend to chance it, Sue; I have but little to lose and much to gain if I succeed."

"Dat am so, Missus. You hab borne dem sorrows like an Angel ob de Lord; and when I tink ob dat Widow, I feel dat I could see her die in her blood and her sins."

"We will take care of her, Sue; she is nearly at the end of her rope. I will make her know who I am before I get through with her."

"Missus, I hab trust in de Lord dis twenty years. He nebber left me to dis day. He fight my battles and deliber me from my enemies. Bress his holy name."

"Sue, I have no desire to hear a sermon to-day."

"Well, Missus, de hand of de Lord is in eberyting, mind dat; and if you speck to gain de day, trust in Him."

"I am not as strong a believer in such things as you are, Sue. I will see if your prophecy comes true or not."

Mrs. B. returned to her sitting-room with Maggie and Willie on each side of her. Willie looked up in his mother's face and said:

"Ain't pa a bad man, ma?"

"What makes you think so, dear?"

"Cause you and Aunt Sue says he is."

"You must not talk so, dear Willie."

"Well, pa says you are a naughty ma."

"You must not repeat what others say, Willie."

"Well, ma, what you say, ain't it dood?"

"Yes, dear."

"Well, you say pa naughty man?"

"Talk of something else, Willie."

"I see pa cole you, ain't he bad?"

Little Maggie looked up with an innocent smile:

"Ma, pa is a dood man?" He brings me cakes and tandy; ain't he dood, ma?"

Mrs. B. looked down upon her little darling with a pleasant smile, but made no reply.

The following evening Peter returned and entered the kitchen.

"Well, hab you got back?" said Sue.

"Yes; I hab; where is Missus?"

"In the sitting room."

Peter hastened in.

"Peter, have you got back?" asked Mrs. B.

"Yes, Missus."

"Well, what is the news at the village?"

"Nofing, Missus."

Peter drew a letter from his pocket and gave it to his mistress.

Mrs. B. glanced at the letter.

"Well, Peter, what questions were asked you at the village?"

"Nofing, Missus."

"Now, Peter, tell me the truth."

"Yes, Missus."

"When your Master returns I don't want you to tell him that I sent you to the village."

"No, Missus."

The letter was from Lawyer Higgins, and was as follows:

Fairfax Village, Aug. 26th.

Dear Madam:—I acknowledge the receipt of your letter, at the hands of your servant, Peter; and after a careful perusal of it, I have become satisfied, provided you can prove the facts, you can obtain a bill. If so, your case is a plain one. Your papers required to be filed, and your witnesses produced upon the day of trial. You desire to know what I will charge you to prosecute your case. I never take a case of that kind for less than three hundred dollars; but, as I have been acquainted with you and your family for a number of years, and believing you to be a lady in the strictest sense of the term, I will obligate myself to secure you a bill for two hundred dollars—a hundred dollars in hand, and the balance when I take the stand to prosecute your case. You can forward me the money by mail or hand, then I will proceed. You are aware that I shall have to give thirty days notice through the columns of some Journal in accordance with the laws of the State. I shall await your answer.

Yours, respectfully,
James Higgins, Atty.

Mrs. B., after reading the counsel's letter, was puzzled to know where to get the money to pay the fees; she hesitated to make a demand on Mr. Oldham, notwithstanding he had offered to assist her. In a few hours, Mrs. H. knocked at her door; she opened it and said:

"Is it possible this is you? Walk in and take a seat."

"I have but a few moments to stop," said Mrs. H. "Having heard that your husband was absent, I concluded to call down and see you. I would not have him see me here for the world."

Mrs. B. smiled and said: "I will protect you; I have got him pretty well cowed down."

"Do tell me how you have been getting along since our last interview?"

"I have made things warm for him, you may depend. After all, I pity him; he is so humble."

"Pity, indeed! He deserves a good thrashing. I am a little inclined to believe that you still love him?"

"No; at the same time it is not unnatural for us to possess humane feelings for those with whom we have been so long identified."

"My time is short as I come on business. Have you employed your counsel?"

"I have just received a letter from Lawyer Higgins relative to the case, and have just finished reading it."

"What does he think of it?"

"He stated in his letter to me, that if I could sustain the charges, there would be no difficulty in obtaining a bill."

"What are his charges?"

"Two hundred dollars. For the life of me I don't know where I can raise the money, as I have none of my own. I hate to write to Mr. Oldham for it. I have no doubt it would come forth."

"You need not write him a single line for money. I have three hundred dollars in my possession that he authorized me to pay over to you."

"'Tis truly a God-send; I am under a thousand obligations to you and the giver. It would have been impossible for me to have raised the amount otherwise. I have made up my mind fully never to ask Brown for a single dollar while breath warms my body."

"I don't think you will ever have any need, as long as Mr. Oldham is your friend."

"To-morrow morning I will forward Lawyer Higgins his entire fee and authorize him to make arrangements for the trial."

"Higgins is a good lawyer; at the same time H. Montgomery would have been my choice. I would not be surprised if Mr. B. employed him against you."

"I will chance Higgins, as I have obligated myself. I wish you to secure all the evidence you can to enable us to succeed. I have misplaced the letter you gave me from Mr. Oldham. I have turned the house upside down and I cannot find it."

"I trust it has not fallen into the hands of your husband. If so, it will ruin us."

"No; I am satisfied he has not got it. If he had it he would have spoken about it. It would be too good a thing for him to keep. I may come across it when I least expect."

"I would like very much to have a consultation with you before the trial comes off. Likewise, so would Martha and Aunt Polly; they feel deeply interested in your behalf."

"I shall endeavor to call at your house to-day two weeks, or perhaps sooner."

"I shall look for you without fail. Mr. Oldham will be delighted when he reads your notice for a bill. He is already crazy about you."

Mrs. B. laughed and said:

"I am glad to hear that somebody thinks well of me."

"And if you should need more money, all you have to do is to name it; he has plenty of it. By the way, I forgot to tell you I saw the Widow in her front yard as I passed."

"Did she speak to you?"

"Speak to me! Indeed the look she gave me was terrible in the extreme."

"I judge she begins to think I am not the fool she took me for. I will be a terror to her before I get through."

"She begins to realize her condition. I guess she wishes she had been more prudent."

"I think so."

"Do you intend to remain here until the trial is over?"

"I do not intend to move a peg. My renegade husband and the Widow wouldn't want a better thing if I should leave. They would feel highly gratified to get rid of me so easy. He has his bed and I have mine. Sue cooks his meals; I have not sat at the table with him for three weeks past. The children and myself eat in the little parlor adjoining the bed-room."

"I judge that he begins to think that you are in earnest. Keep him at his distance and have as little to say to him as possible. Push the matter right through," replied Mrs. H.

"There shall be no delay on my part, I assure you. I also requested Lawyer Higgins to retain for me and the children one-third of the property."

"Dear me! Mr. Oldham is abundantly able to take care of you and the children; we have spoken to him already about them. He was delighted at the idea to become their adopted father."

"That may be all right; but let every man that is able take care of his own children. Mr. B. is fully able, and why not provide for them?"

"That is true. They will be under your care after the trial."

"I don't know; the Court may not assign them to me."

"Nonsense; they would no more think of giving them in his charge than they would to strangers; you have not the slightest idea of the feeling against him. He has no friends. His name is on every tongue, and none speak well of him. You are, indeed, blessed above thousands to have such a friend as Mr. Oldham at this time. It looks as if Providence had ordered it. Does it not?"

"Indeed it does, and were it not for him I don't know what I should do."

"Now, dear, tell me if you succeed in obtaining a bill, do you intend marrying him?"

Mrs. B. laughed and said:

"Nothing short of matrimony will satisfy him; he has been very kind to me."

"Ha! ha! I tell you he is the man for you. I suppose your present companion would have duck-fits if he knew it."

"It is a matter that should be kept strictly private."

"The Widow will use her endeavors to exonerate herself and to defeat us, if possible. She has brought her ducks to a fine market. I believe she would assassinate me if she dare. She is getting desperate."

"I don't fear her."

"I tell you she is not only revengeful but she is indeed a dangerous woman."

"I have always thought so."

"I have a great deal to say in a short space of time, as I must be hurrying off. What disposition will you make of poor Sue, in case you obtain a bill?"

"Sue is my individual property, and I would almost leave one of my children as to leave her. She has long been my faithful servant and adviser in these trying times. She is worthy of my consideration and care. I have become satisfied that Negroes, like other races, know their friends and appreciate them. I have used my endeavors to secure the confidence of Peter, but without effect."

"How is that?"

"When I first came on the farm I took a dislike to him; I must say, without a justifiable cause. I treated him indifferently. He seems never to have forgotten it. He would be of considerable service to me, if it were not for the dislike which I think he entertains for me. He sticks to his Master like a leech."

"I find it is better to use everybody right, however humble in circumstances. There are times when they can be of use. It is better to have their confidence, friendship, influence and esteem, than their dislike. My mother had an old Negro woman who nursed me. We called her Aunt Debby. The children loved her as they did their mother, not withstanding she used to switch us whenever she felt like it. Dear me, I must be off."

"What's your hurry?"

"I have stayed longer than I anticipated. Good-bye, good-bye."

They kissed each other and parted. After Mrs. H. had left, Mrs. B. rushed into the kitchen to inform Sue of her success.

"Missus, did you get de money? Dey say 'one bird in de hand is wort two in de bush.'"

"Yes, Sue; here it is."

"Wall! wall! dat am de fact. I so glad. We are all right now, Missus."

"Yes, Sue; in the morning I shall forward two hundred of it to Lawyer Higgins. If you see old Bob pass, tell him I want to see him. I shall get him to take the money as he is going to the village."

"Missus, do you tink dat darkey can be, 'lied on?"

"Yes, Sue; he is very trustworthy and knows how to keep matters intrusted to him."

"Missus," remarked Sue, "are you gwine to write?"

"No, Sue," replied Mrs. B. "The money is all that is required to commence the suit."

"Well, if you can depend on dat fellow Bob, it is all right."

"Many take old Bob to be a fool, but those who will buy him for one will get cheated; he is a good old Negro, but has his queer ways; and it is not every one that can get along with him."

"Dat am de truft; he am mighty stubborn sometimes."

"Sue, I expect you are a little prejudiced against old Bob, because he don't spark you."

"Ha! ha! For de heben sake hear dat, Missus! Do you tink I would hab dat darkey? No, Missus, I am too high-string for dat."

Mrs. B. roared with laughter. The following morning Bob passed and halted—the road leading to the main road from his Master's farm ran directly through Mr. B.'s plantation. Sue hailed him. He went to the kitchen-door and inquired:

"Whar your Mistruss?"

"She am in de bed-room," replied Sue.

Sue then informed Mrs. B., who came to the door and said:

"Good morning, Robert."

"Sarvant, Missus."

"Bob, I wish you to deliver this package to Lawyer Higgins at the village; be careful not to lose it."

"Yes, Missus; I be sure not to do dat."

"Robert, if you attend to it properly, I may be induced to give you Sue for a wife."

Robert opened his mouth and laughed until the tears ran down his sable cheeks in torrents, and exclaimed to Sue:

"Gal! you is mine as sure as dis darkey am alibe."

"G'long, darkey; who does you tuck me to be? You tink I is some common darkey to hab de likes ob you," said Sue.

The following day Robert returned and presented Mrs. B. with a note enclosed in an envelop from Lawyer Higgins. It read as follows:

Fairfax, Aug. 18th.

Mrs. Brown:

Madam—I avail myself of the present opportunity to inform you that I received two hundred dollars, the entire fee; please accept this as an acknowledgment for the same. I will send a notice tomorrow morning to the *Alexandria Gazette* for publication. Your case will, perhaps, be among the first on the docket. Notify your witnesses of the fact. I will drop you a few lines informing you what day it will come up. Entertain no fears. I shall do the best I can for you. I remain,

Yours, respectfully,
James Higgins.

CHAPTER IV

A short time before the trial Mrs. B. dreamed she saw her brother and mother, who had been dead many years; her brother entered her room first, her mother following, and lastly came in Aunt Polly Hopkins, Martha Lovejoy and Mrs. H. Her mother and brother were clothed in shrouds as white as snow; the last named three were dressed in robes as black as jet; they huddled themselves together in the north corner of the room and looked vicious in the extreme. Mrs. B.'s mother appeared not to notice them. She bent over the bed and kissed her daughter, and stroked back her hair with a hand as cold as ice. She turned to her son and said: "What has possessed these evil spirits to congregate here?" As she spoke thus all of them hung their heads. He pointed to them with the finger of death, and said: "It is they who seek the destruction of my sister, and are conspiring to drag her to that region of misery and desolation." Polly was standing nearest to them. "That spirit," said he, "would destroy us in the twinkling of an eye, if it was not for the guardian angel of heaven." Then said the spirit of Mrs. B.'s mother: "Oh! what wretched beings they must be; how dreadful is sin; it is a terrible curse." As she spoke all of them veiled their faces and said: "Come, let us depart from this; the day is breaking." Aunt Polly threw up her veil as she passed out—her eyes looked like balls of fire. She gave them a terrible look. Then there appeared an angel who said to the spirits of Mrs. B. and her son: "Your time is up!" The two spirits then looked wistfully upon Mrs. B. Her mother again kissed her with her cold lips of death; this awoke her; she found it to be only a dream, but it left a serious impression on her mind. She then thought of the story Sue told her about the spirits.

Mr. B., during his absence, saw in one of the daily papers, his wife's advertisement for a bill; he immediately addressed a letter to H. Montgomery to defend the suit, which was readily accepted.

Winchester, Va., August 31st.

Mr. Brown:

Dear Sir—I take this method to inform you that I have received yours, dated Aug. 27th. In reply to the same, I should be more than happy to act as your counsel. My fee is two hundred and fifty dollars; your word for the amount is sufficient; have your witnesses in readiness to appear at the October Term.

Yours, respectfully,
H. Montgomery.

Mr. B. returned home on the following day, and interrogated his wife in reference to her applying for a bill.

"Sir, your breath is spent in vain," retorted Mrs. B. "I told you from the first I intended to secure a final separation from you, and I intend to be as good as my word."

"Are you sure you will succeed in obtaining a bill?"

"Yes, sir; without the slightest difficulty. You have committed manslaughter upon your own domestic and social happiness. You are looked upon with contempt by all lovers of society. You have shown your hand, and I have called you to an account."

"Madam," he replied, "you are very sanguine of success; be

careful that you don't slip up on it. I have fully made up my mind to defend against you and your tutors. I have thus declared my intention, though it may be cowardice on my part. Nevertheless I have a character to sustain, and he who has not the moral courage to defend his honor, when assailed and pursued by the bloodhounds of society, deserves to be drummed out of a Christian community and stamped with the brand of cowardice. Marshal your legions for the conflict; like the ancient shepherd, I have only the sling of justice and the stone of truth to contend against my enemies, and with a well-directed aim I may be enabled to deal them a death-blow. I am ready for the conflict at any moment. I entertain no fears, and believe I shall achieve a noble victory in behalf of my character. I shall endeavor to leave their mangled bodies upon the field of conflict, as a warning to all peace-disturbers and calumniators."

The following letter was received by Mrs. B. from a lady friend:

Alexandria, August 30th.

Dear Nellie—In scanning over one of our daily papers, much to my surprise and mortification, I saw a notice of your application for a bill of divorce. What in the world has induced you to pursue such a course? I feal that you have been hasty and unthoughtful. It would be far better for you to cover your companion's faults with the veil of charity, than to make your domestic affairs public to the outside world. Who of us are without faults? Such proceedings are not only injurious to yourself, but has its effect upon society. Remember your position, the circle in which you associate, and the example you should set as a pattern for your children. No two joined together in the sacred bonds of wedlock, were ever known to be perfect; and each with an observing eye can detect faults in the other. Do endeavor to settle your difficulties between yourselves; if so, you will choke off public slander which invariably attends such cases. I admonish you as a friend. "He that controlleth his own temper and household, is greater than he that taketh a city." Be wise and prudent; the calumniators of society are only waiting to satisfy their craving appetites; none are exempt from the trials and afflictions of life; they attend us from the cradle to the tomb. Have you thought of the many dangers that attend a lone woman through life, on the right and on the left? Gins and snares are set to entrap her;

the strongest of women have fallen a prey to the fowler. I trust you will give this letter due consideration, before you advance further. This advice is from one that loves you as a sister.

Yours, affectionately,
Maria A. Dangerfield.

Mr. Oldham's letter to Mrs. B:

Greensville, September 15th.

Dear Nellie—I am pleased to inform you that in looking over the *Alexandria Gazette*, I saw a notice setting forth your intention to obtain a bill. It seems that you are resolved to secure justice. I am proud you have the courage. Keep in good spirits. I am your true friend, and whatever means you may need in the future, hesitate not to make it known at once. You are aware that it is necessary for me to keep in the dark for fear of exciting suspicion. I gave Mrs. H. an order the other day for four hundred dollars, three hundred of which amount I ordered her to pay over to you, which I hope you have received before this. I shall be at Mrs. H.'s one week from to-day. I shall be more than happy to meet you there, as I suppose it will be the first and last interview we shall have before the trial comes off. When I contemplate the happiness in store for us, I can scarcely realize the fact. I am anxious for your troubles to end, and to receive you as my lawful and cherished bride. Hoping you will pardon me, if you consider me forward,

Yours truly,
J. O.

Mrs. B.'s reply:

Brown's Farm, September 16th.

Dear Joseph—It is with more than ordinary pleasure that I take my pen in hand to inform you that I received your very welcome letter dated September 15th. I trust these lines will find you in good health and fine spirits, as they leave me. The clouds of despair, gloom, doubt and fear, are fast disappearing. I feel more cheerful and hopeful than ever of late. Matters are progressing finely, and it will be but a short period before we shall love each other more sincerely and devotedly. You must use the utmost discretion, and instead of directing letters in my present name, direct them in the name of *Elizabeth Jackson* in the future. I will inquire for your letters to me by that name. It becomes us to keep matters strictly private. If they should extend beyond our confidence it would be a terrible instrument in the hands of my present husband to be used against us; so far, he is entirely ignorant of our correspondence, and I trust he will be until I accomplish my object. Allow me to thank you kindly for the liberal sum you sent me. I trust you will never have cause to doubt my sincerity, or to question my love and friendship for you. In accordance with your request I shall be at Mrs. H.'s on the day appointed. Don't fail, dear Joseph, to meet me there. I never thought I could ever again become infatuated with a man as I have with you; my affections are concentrated wholly in you. Be hopeful and all will come out right.

Yours, affectionately,
Nellie Brown.

CHAPTER V

According to promise, Mrs. B. went on the day appointed for the meeting to the house of Mrs. H. On arriving there she found all present, except her intended, Mr. Joe Oldham. Aunt Polly, Martha and Mrs. H. gave her a cordial welcome.

"Dear me, child," said Aunt Polly, "how have you been? I haven't seen you since our first meeting. I have heard of your progress through Mrs. H. and Martha. I was pleased to hear that you are still on the war-path."

"I have been quite well, I thank you, though I have had many trials since I last saw you. I am fully determined to carry it through—sink or swim, perish or survive," replied Mrs. B.

"I admire your pluck. The time is not far distant when you will receive your just reward, and come out as gold tried in the fire—a free and independent woman."

"She would make a good soldier," said Martha, laughing.

"Thank you for the compliment," said Mrs. B.

During the conversation, Mr. Oldham entered. The party seemed delighted to greet and welcome him. He threw his arms around Mrs. B. and kissed her; she blushed, but soon became apparently easy.

"How have you been, Nellie? I have long wanted to see you," said Mr. Oldham.

Mrs. B., with a pleasant smile, answered:

"I have been well, but have had a sea of troubles since I was here last; and if it was not for poor Sue, I think I would have sank under them."

"Sue has been your comforter?"

"Yes; she has stuck to me like a mother."

"I supposed that you were having a tough time of it."

"Poor thing, she is to be pitied. I know what such troubles are. I have been married myself five times," said Aunt Polly.

Mrs. B. laughed excessively, and said:

"You are an old hand at the bellows then?"

"Yes, I can blow and strike at the same time."

This remark set them all laughing.

"You never failed to secure a bill from your husbands when they failed to comply with their obligations."

"I have long made it an established rule to quit them then and there. I was not particular as to a bill. In some cases I have taken leg bail instead of a bill. You know, child, the world is wide, and in it is plenty of room; I have never employed a lawyer to my knowledge, nor do I think I ever shall. There never has been a law during the history of my life to compel a woman to live with a man that she did not love."

"That's pretty good, Aunt Polly. I think the women ought to subscribe for a medal for you. We had better now proceed to business as the time is short, and I have a considerable distance to go. Nellie, what counsel have you employed?" asked Mr. Oldham.

"Lawyer Higgins; are you acquainted with him?"

"By reputation; I have seen him once or twice, and have heard that he is a good counsellor."

"He is. At the same time I told Mrs. B. I preferred H. Montgomery. He is a 'pealer,'" said Mrs. H.

"I think it would have been better to make sure work of it by employing him. However, it is too late now; it is time that we should prepare for the coming conflict, and have our witnesses in readiness. How many witnesses can we muster?" asked Mr. Oldham.

"Myself, Martha and Aunt Polly are all I know of at present," returned Mrs. H.

"Two is as good as a thousand, if they can establish the facts connected with the case."

"I think I am in possession of those facts."

"My evidence will go a good way towards convicting him," said Martha.

"If I don't convict him I will scare him terribly, depend on it. I have heard enough of the gentleman to hang an ordinary man if made known. I shall not hesitate to tell all I have heard," responded Aunt Polly.

"We have got much the best of him. I never engage in jobs of this kind unless I have the advantage and the longest end of the rope."

"I am sure we can succeed if the witnesses will hang together on the main points. It is likely the Widow will be introduced as a witness against us. I have heard that he has one or two others. I have not learned who they are. Like a drowning man, he will catch at anything to save himself," replied Mrs. B.

"His witnesses will do him but little good. If he knows what is best for him, he would never enter the Court House door," said Mrs. H.

"I don't really believe that he will defend the suit," responded Martha.

"He never will give it up without a struggle for victory. The least said about this matter the better. I am willing to advance whatever money that is required to carry the case through. I consider it a success," remarked Mr. Oldham.

"Indeed you may," replied Mrs. H.

"If we don't succeed," said Aunt Polly, "I will lose my head."

"Ha! ha!"

"We cannot fail."

"Mrs. H. and Mrs. B. I wish to have a private interview with you for a few moments," said Mr. Oldham.

"Certainly," they replied, excusing themselves to Aunt Polly and Martha, and entered the dining-room.

"Nellie," remarked Mr. Oldham, "perhaps this will be the last time that we shall be enabled to see each other before the trial comes off. I think it likely that you may need more money, and for fear that we may not meet soon, I present you with five one hundred dollar bills."

"Dear me, this is intruding on good nature," answered Mrs. B.

Mrs. H. gave her a nudge with her arm to silence her.

"Not at all."

He also gave Mrs. H. three fifty dollar bills to divide with Martha and Aunt Polly. They thanked him kindly; he kissed Mrs. B good-bye, and requested her to write to him soon.

After Mr. Oldham had left, Mrs. H. said:

"He has the biggest heart of any little man I ever saw."

She then asked Aunt Polly and Martha:

"What do you think he gave us?"

"I have no idea," replied Aunt Polly.

"I am sure I have not," said Martha.

"He gave Mrs. B. five one hundred dollar bills, and also three fifty dollar bills to me to divide among the three of us."

"Ha! ha! He is a gentleman and he shall be rewarded," said Aunt Polly.

"Is it a fact?" asked Martha. "I am a little astonished at his liberality, though I knew that he was generous. As I said before, 'love has no price,' and well may he love a woman like you, Mrs. B."

Mrs. B. smiled and said:

"I have become accustomed to your flattery."

"Indeed it is true," said Mrs. H. "If I was as handsome as yourself, I would play the men a merry string."

"She knows that she is handsome without telling her," added Aunt Polly.

"I must be off," said Mrs. B.

"What is your hurry? Will you not stay to tea," inquired Mrs. H.

"Thank you; I have to walk, and it is better that I should start early."

"Why did you not ride Bet?"

"To tell you the truth, I had no desire to see my friend, the Widow. If I rode, I would be compelled to pass her house."

"I would give myself little trouble about her; I could ride over her and not speak to her."

Mrs. H. laughed and said:

"That's like you, Martha."

"Friends," said Mrs. B. "you have been exceedingly kind to me, and I am better prepared to reward you, than I thought I would be. Will one hundred dollars more satisfy you?"

"Oh dear me, don't rob yourself," replied Mrs. H.

"Tell her to accept the hundred dollars," Aunt Polly said to Martha, in an undertone.

Mrs. B. bid them good-bye, and desired to hear from them at the earliest opportunity.

"If that woman is defeated in getting a bill, Oldham will kill you," remarked Martha to Mrs. H.

"Pray, what will he do with you?" asked Mrs. H.

"I come in for an equal share; but have had little to say at this gathering. I pity her and would be delighted to see her succeed; but to tell you the truth, I don't think that she has any better show to obtain a bill than I have to be Queen of England," said Martha.

"Business is business," said Aunt Polly. "We make our living by it. We should have no sympathy. It is our duty to seize our victims wherever we can find them, and have no scruples; money is what we are after!"

Mrs. H. laughed and said:

"Your head is clear, Aunt Polly."

"The afterpart is what I dread—that is being brought into Court. Those lawyers are very personating and impudent," replied Martha.

"If you get paid for it, why complain? You must learn not to care or fear even Satan. Courage is what you need," said Aunt Polly.

Readers, we will now return to Mrs. B. She arrived home apparently gratified with her prospects. She told Sue of her success, and the amount she had received from Mr. Oldham, and charged her to keep it a secret.

"Missus, did you get de money?"

Mrs. B. drew from her pocket the bills, and said, "Sue, there it is. I intend, after the suit, to buy you a handsome present."

"Tank you, Missus, you am fixed. Am you gwine to marry dat gentleman?"

"Sue, that is a question to answer," with a shrug of her shoulders. "How would you like to have him for your master?"

"Don no; dese men are very unsartin, Missus. If you gwine to be married, youd better gib me my *free papers*."

"What in the world has come over you, Sue? What a strange idea! What do you want to be free for, Sue?"

"Well, Missus; you see you might dies, and dey might send me down Souf. If I is free dey can't sell me den, Missus."

"Sue, do you know there is more free Negroes now than can take care of themselves?"

"Don no, Missus; I tink freedom am very good for eberybody."

"Don't talk so simple, Sue; you would starve to death inside of two weeks."

"I speck not, Missus. I am got two good hands; nebber starve as long as I can work, Missus."

During the conversation Mr. B. came in, walked to the sitting-room and seated himself on the sofa. Mrs. B. passed to and fro in the room several times, he taking little or no notice of her. At last she inquired:

"I have one question to ask you, sir."

"What is that?"

"Do you intend to oppose me in obtaining a bill?"

"Madam, I am done discussing the matter; you seek invariably to drag me into a controversy. I told you I would defend my character as long as there was an enemy who assailed it; and I tell you again, for the last time, until we meet face to face in the Court House, I will never allow myself to be taken a prisoner by those friends of yours without making a good fight."

"You will be sick of it, mark my words. If you knew what was best for you, you would leave the State and never show your face in it again."

"That is your opinion. I am one of those who never run; not am I easily scared."

Mr. B. intended making a visit to his old home at Richmond, to see his parents and to remain there until the time for the trial to come off. He prepared himself for the journey, and ordered Sue to have breakfast early, and Peter to pack his valise and have Queen saddled. Also a horse for himself, as he wished Peter to accompany him to the village.

On the following morning everything was in readiness at the appointed time. Before starting, Mr. B entered the room of his wife and kissed each of his children good-bye. He then returned to the kitchen, and told Sue to take good care of the little ones, and bade her good-bye. He desired Peter to bring Queen back, as he intended to take the stage at Fairfax.

Peter and his Master arrived at Fairfax Village the same afternoon. Peter concluded to go part of the way home that night. His Master remarked to him:

"Peter, take good care of everything until I return."

"Yes, sar."

His Master gave him a twenty dollar gold piece, and bade him good-bye.

Peter arrived home the following afternoon. His Mistress asked him what his Master had to say about matters and things generally. Peter hesitated to tell.

"Peter, I want you to tell me the truth."

"Well, Missus, he speck you am gwine to try to get de bill."

"Did he say what he expected would be the result?"

"No, Missus; he says he am gwine to make dem sick ob it."

"Ha! ha! We will see about that. Peter, I want you to go to the post office and inquire if there is a letter for me."

Peter went and inquired for a letter for Mrs. B. He got one, and returned and gave it to her. She opened it in haste, and glanced over it. It was from her counsellor, Lawyer Higgins, notifying her that her case was set for the 15th day of October. Also, requesting her to have her witnesses in Court on that day.

After receiving the letter from Lawyer Higgins, Mrs. B. dispatched the following to Mr. Oldham:

Brown's Farm, Sept. 25th.

Dear Josey:—I hope these lines will find you enjoying good health as they leave me. I am pleased to inform you that 'my lord' left for Richmond day before yesterday. I should be happy to have you make me a visit during his absence. At the same time, 'discretion is the better part of valor.' Peter, I am satisfied, would sell us at any price. He is his Master's pet Negro; he is a tattler, and I dare not trust him. I hope all things will work for our good. I received a letter from Lawyer Higgins, notifying me that the trial is set for the 15th day of October next. You will do me a kind favor if you will inform Aunt Polly, Mrs. H. and Martha that my case is set for that day. As they are the principal witnesses I wish them to prepare for it, and secure all others that can assist in the matter. My dear, you will excuse this short and brief letter. My mind is so unsettled that I scarcely know what to do. I hope you will not regard my love growing languid or cold to you. Circumstances prevent me from writing you as interesting a letter as I would wish. In nineteen or twenty days, I expect to receive an honorable discharge from Brown. Then, dear Joe, I expect to re-enlist with you for life. Be hopeful, and remember the "darkest hour is said to be about the break of day." Write me a *genuine* love letter.

Yours, affectionately,
Nellie Brown.

Mr. Oldham replied as follows:

Greensville, September 27th.

Dear Nellie—I am delighted to acknowledge the receipt of your very flattering letter dated the 25th inst. I have scarcely slept a night since our last interview. You are constantly in my mind. If you should be defeated in securing a bill, I am forever a ruined and wrecked man. I am truly a slave to the passion of love. However strange it may appear to you, it is nevertheless true. I have the utmost confidence in your pledge and esteem for me; at the same time we are changeable creatures; I trust you will be true to your obligation. I shall commence, dear Nellie, preparing for your reception, and contemplate on our future bliss. According to your request, I shall notify Aunt Polly, Martha, and Mrs. H. to appear on the day appointed. If they can prove what they have said they knew of the affair, the victory is ours.

Yours, affectionately,
Joseph Oldham.

Mrs. B., on reading the foregoing letter, felt hurt at Oldham's doubts as to her sincerity, and wrote the following reply:

Brown's Farm, Sept. 29.

Dear Josey—I received your letter, dated the [27th], and be assured that it surprised me. You seem to express yourself strangely. Have I given you any just cause to doubt me? Have not my letters to you been warm and affectionate? I am no coquette nor pretender of love and friendship, unless I am convinced that those whom I bestow it upon will cherish it. I have not been unmindful of my pledge to you, Dear Josey. I fear you have allowed some babbler, at an unguarded moment, to whisper evil in your ears. I shall prove them to be false. If such is the case, I shall look to the day when the sunshine of peace shall linger around my pathway, and when you and I shall be the idols of each other. Let not such ideas haunt you. The golden pleasures of life are too precious to be lost. Let us improve each passing hour. I hope, my dear, this letter will ease your troubled breast, and disperse all doubts and fears. Keep a good heart. You stated in your letter to me, that you were making all the necessary preparations for my reception. I am glad to hear it. I hope success may attend our efforts. Keep things quiet.

Yours, affectionately,
Nellie Brown.

CHAPTER VI

The long looked-for day drew near for the final settlement of the case. Mrs. B. made all necessary arrangements on the 13th day of October. On the following morning she ordered Peter to saddle Bet, and requested him to accompany her to the village. She bade Sue good-bye, kissed the children, and started. They arrived at Fairfax about three o'clock in the afternoon. As she rode down Main street she saw Mr. B., much to her surprise, conversing with Lawyer Montgomery in front of the American Hotel. She said to Peter:

"There is your master."

Peter seemed delighted to get a glimpse of him once more. They put up at the Washington Hotel, then kept by Mr. W———. As she rode up, he brought out a chair and assisted her off. She ordered dinner for herself and servant, and food for the horses. Peter led them around to the barn and saw them amply provided for. He then hastened up the road to greet his master. As he approached his master seemed equally delighted to meet him and extended his hand.

"Well, Peter, I see that your mistress has come."

"Yes, sah; she am here; she would hab me come along wid her."

"That is all right, Peter; it is your duty to obey her orders."

"Yes, sah."

"How are the children and Sue?"

"Dey is fine, Massa."

"When do you intend starting for home?"

"In de morning, Massa."

"I have some things I wish you to carry home to the children; call here this afternoon and get them."

"Yes, sar."

"Tell Sue to take good care of the babes; I will be home in a few days."

"Yes, sar."

He and his Master parted.

The following morning, about eight o'clock, the Widow rode into town on horseback, accompanied by Mr. Nye. Two hours later Aunt Polly, Mrs. H. and Martha also arrived, seated in an ox-wagon, just as the names of the witnesses were called. They had scarcely time to arrange their toilets. By this time the other witnesses were already in Court, which was crowded to its utmost capacity. It was not long before Aunt Polly entered the Court House. Her disciples following her. They were the centre of attraction.

After the examination of the witnesses, Lawyer Higgins closed his case on behalf of his client, as follows:

May it please the Court and you, Gentlemen of the Jury—This case is one of vast interest and importance. It involves the liberty, the peace, and the happiness of my client, Mrs. B. The law, as I understand it, is to protect the weak against the encroachments of the strong. Society, morality and virtue need to be fostered and protected. He who destroys virtue wounds society, and deserves to be punished to the full extent of the law. Woman is a weak vessel, and should be shielded against the attacks of men who disregard the marriage vow—who violate its rights with impunity and trample under foot those whom they have sworn before heaven's altar to cherish and protect. If justice is the right of the weak, in common with the strong, it is the duty of this Court to act unbiassed and to give justice to whom it is due. I shall, gentlemen of the jury, for the satisfaction of this Court, convince you of the guilt of Mr. B., who might have been a pattern of society, and a congenial companion. But, like many others, he had suffered himself to be drawn into the net of vice, and the snares of crime. The Widow, I have no doubt, was once the idol of society. At an unguarded moment she yielded to the tempter, and thus brought disgrace to her own door. I sympathise for her, and hope she is not beyond redemption. We are creatures of circumstances and are liable to err. At the same time I am not here to defend her nor to excite sympathy in her behalf—she is a woman. But gentlemen, it would be far better for the peace and tranquillity of society, if persons like her were transported beyond the boundaries of enlightened civilization. I have every reason to believe, according to the evidence, that she is a dangerous woman, who hesitates not to corrupt the pure and the good. Mr. B. has brought dishonor to his home. The evidence introduced here is truthful and reliable. The circumstances surrounding the case would leave little, if any, doubt in the mind of the jurors, that Mr. B. is thrice guilty. Many have been convicted upon circumstantial evidence, but the evidence introduced here, gentlemen of the jury, is *prima facie*—the chain of evidence given by Martha, Mrs. Hopkins and Mrs. H. is a unit; his visits day after day at the Widow's house, is sufficient itself to satisfy this Court that there was something "rotten in Denmark;" but, gentlemen of the jury, there is another fact that I wish to impress upon your minds, though it may not be considered evidence according to our law. At the same time, it has its bearing, and shows clearly that Mr. B's conduct has long been suspected. That is, the various reports, (degrading as they may be) have again, and again been sounded in the ears of Mrs. Hopkins and the lady who was formerly known as Mrs. Martha Lovejoy, derogatory to the character of Mr. B. Gentlemen of the jury, look upon the lovely face of Mrs. B., and, if you are judges of human nature, you can see innocence beaming from her countenance, and say with me—"Pity in the extreme that a lady of her education, refinement, and disposition is thus sacrificed by the man who claims to be her benefactor." He is beyond the reach of hope and mercy, and has forfeited every claim upon this good and virtuous woman. She sits here, clothed in spotless garments of purity. The marriage contract, though a civil contract and a mutual obligation, the relationship between man and wife should hold them in the bonds of affection as long as each faithfully complied with the duties attached to the sacred rites. I have no doubt the learned counsel for the defence will soar aloft upon the wings of imagination, and will undoubtedly enchant you with his eloquent oratory, aiming to impeach the credibility of the witnesses for the plaintiff. The law of holy writ denounces fornication as a heinous sin; and the law of our common country has long been a terror to those who violate the marriage vow. It is your duty, gentlemen of the jury, to come to the rescue of virtue, and to sustain morality. Sin is sweeping through our land like a tornado, threatening to demolish the great temple of society, and to sweep to the bosom of destruction the weak and the timid. Everywhere we see the effects of sin, and its fearful results. Let us not, as watchmen upon the walls of society, close our eyes to these facts, but unite as one man in cherishing its growth and progress. We have wives, and many of us are raising children. For what? I trust not for vice, crime and disgrace. No! no! God forbid. For the good of society—may they ever be its ornaments, and the priceless jewels of our hearts. Gentlemen of the jury, I have said sufficient, I trust, including the evidence, to induce you, if free from prejudice, to render a just decision for Mrs. B. She is a wronged woman. Upon your decision, gentlemen of the jury, depends her future. There is a higher Court whose Judge is a judge of all living, and before whose august bar the world shall sooner or later stand to be judged for deeds committed on this earth. Think of it, gentlemen of the Jury. Consign her not to a grave of despair nor a valley of gloom. Sustain a feeble woman in her rights. In conclusion, we have had but one witness introduced against us, Mr. Nye. What, if you please, is his evidence? He tells the Court that on or about July 28th or August 1st, he had business at Mrs. H.'s house. As he neared her house he tells you he heard strange voices there. His curiosity became so great that he crept stealthily around the house and stole quietly into her kitchen, as only a thief would do, to pry into matters that did not concern him. He tells you here that he did not see the faces of the parties, but heard the name of Mrs. B. mentioned in connection with Mr. Oldham. Does this evidence establish the guilt of Mrs. B.? Do you not remember, gentlemen of the jury, of reading an account of a murder in New York City in 1847, on the 28th day of August. This murder occurred in a front room on the first floor. A citizen happened (at the time the difficulty occurred) to be passing; he saw the murderer plunge his dagger deep into the heart of the victim. His evidence was ruled out on the ground that he saw the tragedy through a glass window. Now gentlemen of the jury, if the evidence was ruled out—the witness in the case, seeing it in the broad sunlight of day—I ask should not the evidence of Mr. Nye be discarded, who saw not the parties at all? According to his evidence any of us are liable to be convicted of crimes that transgressors may commit, if they have a voice similar to ours. I judge he can designate every resident of Virginia at the dead hour of night by their voices. If we are defeated, I shall look forward to the day when virtue shall receive its just reward, and men of pure hearts and clean hands will not hesitate to shield woman against the cunning deception of man. Give us a society untainted with corruption, and courts that hesitate not to punish crime. Gentlemen of the jury, if you entertain respect for the defendant, you must not allow it to fetter your verdict nor deter justice. Act impartially. If so, the great temple of our society will not fall, but will stand a lasting monument until this great nation has passed away. Will you assist me in defending society and the pure from the devices of the wicked? Let this Court make an example of all such men as Brown. I ask simple justice for the good of society. It is your duty, your right and your sworn obligation, to give justice to whom it is due. She is as innocent and as pure from intrigue as an angel of light, and as free from deception as a bird that drifts in the Summer breeze. The evidence against her is no evidence at all. Give her hope of future bliss and deliver her from the dark and cheerless depths of gloom and despair. And may she realize by your impartial decision the radiant sunlight of joy, hope and happiness. I now leave this case with you, gentlemen of the jury, knowing you to be the advocates of justice, the defenders of virtue, and the friends of good society. You can but free her from him who has blasted her every hope and paralyzed her affections. To you, Mr. Brown, I would say: "Oh! that some invisible power, some angel of light, would dart from the realms of everlasting day and warn you of your wicked condition."

CHAPTER VII

After Mrs. B's counsel had concluded, Lawyer Montgomery began his defence for the defendant, Mr. B., which was as follows:

May it please the Court, and you, Gentlemen of the Jury—I have listened attentively to the learned counsel for plaintiff, Mr. Higgins. He has failed to argue the case from any stand-point. I am the sworn sentinel of justice. It is my duty to guard well every outlet of society, as well as its avenues. I shall this day hew to the line, let the chips fly in whose face they may. I shall aim to throw behind their fortifications of falsehood the red hot shot of truth, and to force the enemy, if possible, to open combat. I am ready for a fair fight. I will seek to take no undue advantages. I shall argue the law upon its merits. Law is as old as God, and stood between Adam and his Maker when the creature violated it. Justice demanded a propitiation. The learned counsellor has endeavored to create and excite sympathy in behalf of plaintiff, Mrs. B. Law is stern and inflexible. It has no sympathy, and he or she who violates its rights incurs its wrath. If my client is guilty of the crime alleged against him, he deserves its punishment. I agree with the learned counsellor in one particular, that society is the great temple of our social and domestic happiness, and the pure worship at its sacred shrine. Knock out its stupendous pillars and desecrate its sacred altars, and that hour the sun of morality, progress and literature sets forever on this nation. This party, gentlemen of the jury, is a base band of conspirators, combined together to make war upon society, and, if possible, to poison its pure streams and overturn its mighty pillars. But, gentlemen, justice is swift on their heels. I see guilt pictured deep in their countenances. It is a great mystery to me that Aunt Polly, as she is called, cannot see it. She has four eyes. Being one of the conspirators, of course, she cannot see it. I shall scourge them to the quick with the lash of Truth and the rod of Justice. I will show this Court who these women are, and their veracity for truth.

[You could have lit a candle in their faces at this moment.]

Mr. Montgomery continued:

Gentlemen of the Jury—You have heard the evidence of Aunt Polly, the great soothsayer, Martha Lovejoy and Mrs. H. The evidence of Mrs. H is the strongest link in the chain, and what is it? She saw Mr. B. and the Widow sitting side by side on an open porch, at noon-day. I ask the Court, is it a crime for a lady and a gentleman to sit side by side? If there is any law touching this point, I know it not. If there is, I would prefer taking up my abode among heathens—behind the bright and glorious sun of civilization. But she comes into the Court and says that things looked very suspicious. To the like of her, I have no doubt it does; she is as corrupt and as base as ever any woman was. Like the Samaritan woman whom our Savior interrogated at the well; she has had many husbands, and the one she now has is not her lawful husband. What is the evidence of Mrs. Martha Lovejoy? She comes into Court with a long and incredible story. And what does it amount to? She says that she has heard so and so, and saw Mr. B. at the Widow's house on several occasions. When asked what she saw—she saw nothing. That is pretty evidence to be introduced into our Courts to convict parties of unimpeachable character! What is her character? She is the vilest of the vile—roaming from house to house, seeking whom she may devour. She is one of those disciples who believe that a woman has the right to set aside the marriage vows at any time, and become the wife of another. She is not to be believed on oath. The last, but not the least, is this Aunt Polly. She is the chief of sinners, and the arch-fiend of despair. She tells you what she has heard—she says she saw nothing. Who can fathom the depths of her crimes—the deception and artfulness she is capable of exerting? The State's prison has long been robbed of its victim; it should have been her residence for the good and peace of society. She has also had her complement of husbands, and is a terror wherever she can make a raid upon the innocent and virtuous.

At this point, Lawyer Montgomery asked that Aunt Polly be called to the stand to answer questions he proposed to ask her.

The Court assented and ordered her to take the stand.

"Aunt Polly?"

"Sir."

"Are you acquainted with J. Oldham?"

"Slightly."

"Do you not know of a certain sum being offered for the separation of Mr. and Mrs. B. by that individual?"

She paused.

"Remember you are sworn to tell the whole truth and nothing but the truth. Answer this question?"

"I did hear Mr. Oldham say that he sympathized with Mrs. B."

"That is not the question. I want to know if you were not present when a certain sum of money was offered for the separation of Mr. and Mrs. B.?"

"I heard Mrs. H. say that she expected to get some money. Cannot recollect whether she named the parties or not."

"You appear to be very hard to make understand. Did you not receive twenty-five dollars from Mrs. B. for services rendered?"

Aunt Polly was struck dumb.

"Answer the question."

"Mrs. H. gave me that amount."

"What did she give it to you for?"

"A present, sir."

"Gentlemen of the Jury, you can see clearly that the truth is yet to be told. This woman is a liar by instinct and education. She is a terrible wretch to contend with. I will prove her before I get through, to be the mother of falsehood. She had rather lie on six months credit than to tell the truth for cash. She says Mrs. H. gave her the money as a present. For the satisfaction of the Court, I wish to recall Horace Nye on the stand again."

The judge called Mr. Nye to the stand.

"Mr. Nye, please make your statement again to the Court what you know about this matter, and answer any questions the counsellor may ask you," said the Judge.

Mr. Nye then made the following statement:

"I called at the house of Mrs. H., according to the best of my knowledge, on business on or about the latter part of July or the first of August. As I neared the house, I heard several strange voices in the sitting-room. After listening a few moments, I became interested in the conversation. I left the front and crept quietly along to the kitchen, which is on the south side, to get a better opportunity of hearing. The kitchen door was ajar. There was no light in the kitchen. I entered and secreted myself behind the door leading to the sitting-room. I heard Mr. Oldham asked Aunt Polly, 'Do you think Mrs. B. loves me?' She told him, 'Yes.' He then asked if she thought they would be successful in aiding her to obtain a bill. She said there was not the least doubt of it."

Mr. Higgins asked the witness what was his business there?

Objected to by Lawyer Montgomery.

Objection sustained by the Court.

Mr. Nye proceeded:

"I heard Mr. Oldham say that he loved her as dearly as his own life, and that money was no object if they could only secure her a bill."

Lawyer Montgomery then proceeded with his argument, as follows:

Gentlemen of the Jury—There is the secret. [Mrs. B. wept like a child.] There are characters brought here to swear away a man's reputation, and destroy his domestic peace and happiness. Money, gentlemen, and an outside lover, are the causes of Mrs. B.'s unhappiness. Now, gentlemen of the jury, I will prove the fact more satisfactory before I get through. It is not uncommon for women, however good, to become corrupted when thrown in contact with such characters as Martha Lovejoy, Aunt Polly and Mrs. H. Those loop-holes through which women leap must be closed—the marriage rights protected and honored. Those peace-disturbers should be made to know that they will not be tolerated. Nor shall they, as long as I have a voice, corrupt society. The evidence of Mr. Nye alone should be sufficient to satisfy you of the falsehoods of these three demons in human shape. Mr. Nye's character for veracity and truth is unimpeachable. Those sharks who prey upon the community should be shunned as vipers. They are as corrupt as the angels of darkness. It should be stamped upon their foreheads with letters of living light, that all may read: "Beware of those vampires of society, those messengers of despair."

Mr. Montgomery here requested that Mrs. H. should be put again on the witness stand to answer a few questions.

The Court granted the request and ordered Mrs. H. to come forward, which she did.

"Mrs. H., are you not acquainted with Mr. Oldham?"

"Great heavens!" she exclaimed and rushed for the door.

The officer intercepted her.

"You leper of society, I have long heard of your notoriety and the deception you have long practised on the community. You are putrified and smell in the nostrils of society. You are a beautiful subject to sit in judgment upon others. Go! As did Naman of old, wash and be healed of your malady. Answer the question?"

Mr. Higgins, counsel for the plaintiff, objected.

The Judge overruled the objection.

Mrs. H. replied, in a trembling voice:

"Y-e-s, sir."

"Did you not take the contract to separate Mr. and Mrs. B. for a certain sum of money?"

She fell to the floor as if shot with a rifle ball.

Mr. Higgins said, "Raise her to her feet."

"I will aim to throw the harpoon of Truth still deeper in this wretch of misery."

They tried to resuscitate her.

"Let her be," said Mr. Montgomery. "I trust she has received a death-wound already. I will call the other conspirator—Martha Lovejoy. Excuse me, madam, as I am not acquainted with your other title since *you* have been divorced."

"Sir!"

"Are you not acquainted with Mr. Oldham?"

"Slightly, sir."

"Do you not know of a certain sum having been paid to Mrs. H. in hand for the separation of Mr. B. and his wife? Remember Ananias and Sapphira who fell dead at the feet of the Prophet for lying. Answer the question."

"I cannot say I do."

"Was you not present when Mr. Oldham paid the money?"

"I did not see the money paid."

"Did you not receive a portion of the sum?"

She paused and answered:

"Mrs. H. paid me a bill she owed me."

"For what?"

Mr. Higgins objected to this.

The Judge sustained him.

"I have the biggest set of perjurers to contend with to-day that ever entered a Court house."

Gentlemen of the Jury—It is an evident truth that the testimony given by those parties is anything but creditable. They have come into Court with lies upon their lips and revenge in their hearts. They have come to strip my client of every earthly hope. Take from a man his bosom companion and his offspring—you take his all, and leave him a total wreck upon life's troubled ocean, without a compass or a rudder to steer his frail bark. Gentlemen of the jury, cypher this case down to yourselves. It is then you will be better able to render a just decision against the conspirators who have banded to undermine the foundations of society, and to swear away the character of that worthy Widow, and to blast her hopes of future happiness. Her earthly all has been stricken down by the hand of death. I ask you, gentlemen of the jury, shall she leave this Court covered with disgrace or in spotless robes of chastity and purity, as in the past? Could her companion speak from the tomb, he would tell you that she is a Christian, and that her persecutors receive their mission from the fiend who made war upon the saints of heaven, and were hurled over its battlements and confined in some unknown place in God's universe. I take back a part of that, gentlemen of the jury. Aunt Polly and her craft know his where-abouts. I will soon submit this case to you for your serious consideration, trusting from the evidence and its credibility that you will be able to render a fair and impartial decision. Gentlemen of the jury, you have heard the evidence for the plaintiff and the defendant. It is for you to determine the guilt or the innocence of my client. But for the satisfaction of this Court, I will show you the depravity of a woman who is said to be a lady, a virtuous and a prudent woman. I will now, gentlemen, read you a letter that she had not the slightest idea was in the possession of her husband.

Mrs. B. exclaimed:

"I am a ruined woman."

He read the letter. The Court resounded with applause. This letter was from Mr. Oldham to Mrs. B., their first correspondence. He then continued:

This is the great secret which has caused this domestic war. I ask you, gentlemen of the jury, is it not an outrage? I wish that Mr. Oldham was here present, I would give him the severest scathing that ever [a] man had. He is a miserable wretch, a fiend of despair, and deserves to be quartered alive. It is not uncommon for women, when they become infatuated with others, to seize any pretext to justify them in their guilt and deceptions. Let us throw up an impregnable bulwark to protect the just from the machinations of the corrupt. This involves the marriage rite; also the character of a gentleman that has stood heretofore unimpeachable in society, and whom I believe to be perfectly innocent of the charges proferred against him to-day. Let him go forth from this Court clothed with all the dignity of manhood and with no blot upon his character. This case, remember gentlemen, involves the happiness of Mr. B. and a rite we hold sacred. The marriage rite, whether a Divine or a civil contract, is binding on those who assume its obligations. It is sanctioned by heaven. They who violate its rights are not the friends of society. It is the foundation of happiness to those who honor it. It is the agency of virtue and morality. It raises woman to that level for which God created her. I appeal to you, gentlemen of the jury, and ask when the ties that bind man and wife together are riven by the influence of such characters as Aunt Polly, Martha Lovejoy and Mrs. H., whose occupation it is to corrupt society and to ensnare the innocent in their gins of vice. Where is the remedy to protect society, and to shield the good against the attacks of the wicked? It should be found here. It is for you and every well-wisher to build up an impregnable wall around society, so high that the wolves may not ascend it, and inscribe upon its stupendous pillars in characters bright and vivid, that all may read it, "None but the good dwell here." Wedlock is the sun that lights up our moral sky, and points us to future greatness and grandeur as a nation. Christianity will lose its virtue and power. The night of heathenism will have spread its gloomy mantle over the radiant skies of our fond hopes and cherished institutions. As long, gentlemen of the jury, as reason keeps her throne, and I have a voice, I will ever defend the just against the attacks of the unjust. Heaven grant that I may ever prove to be the friend and advocate of Truth. Men and women may disguise it and crush it to the earth. It will rise again in its strength and beauty. Why, gentlemen of the jury? Because God is its Divine author. Thousands have become martyrs because they dared to utter it. They rejoiced to die in its defence. I believe when time and eternity shall shake hands—when the mighty nations of earth are entombed in the great sepulchre of time—when earth and sea shall give up their dead—Justice and Truth will be Heaven's brightest attributes. Let us, as Christians, fear God and obey his teachings. I have detained the Court longer than I expected. Hoping that you will bear with me a few moments longer, I wish now to address my remarks to Aunt Polly and her wicked disciples. Aunt Polly! The silvery hairs of your head denote that you have lived nearly your allotted days. You are fast ripening for the grave, and must soon become an inhabitant of the spirit world. You should be the last one engaged in so wicked a scheme. You are gliding down the hill of life. You are standing upon the very verge of eternity. Your life has been spent in vice and crime. I fear Satan has already secured a Bill of Sale of your wicked soul. Oh! that God in his mercy may save you from that death that never dies. Seek favor to-day of God. Do you not know God abhors the slanderer, the liar, the back-biter and the enemies of morality? He will visit them, not in mercy but in wrath. Those who seek to destroy the happiness of their fellow-beings are as much to be dreaded as the angels of night. Well may tears course down your cheeks. I trust they are signs of repentance. Heaven pity you! Mrs. H., you are a wicked and malicious woman. The recording angel of heaven blushes to record your sins. You are as wily as a fox. Your depth of crime is hard to fathom. You are as treacherous as a serpent and as destructive as a wild beast. Well may you blush and hang your guilty head. You have lost every trait that characterizes and adorns woman as the loveliest of creation. Love, purity and goodness are strangers to you. You have not one redeeming trait of character. "Who shall enter the Kingdom of Heaven? She that hath clean hands and a pure heart." You have wronged this just Widow to-day, and have sought to cover her with shame and disgrace. You have wounded her soul. You have sought by stratagem and device to tear asunder man and wife. But I have implicit confidence in the integrity of this jury to protect her and him from the pit which you, Aunt Polly and Martha have dug for them. The time has come that a fearful example should be made of such pests and renegades as you have proven yourselves to be. I hope, gentlemen of the jury, you may never again be called upon to witness such a vile combination of corruptionists and perjurers as have presented themselves here to-day. I leave you, Mrs. H., in the hands of a just God. Martha, you are young in years but old in crime. You might have been an ornament to society, and exerted a good influence in behalf of the community. Your very nature is sinful and wicked. You are in the wrong path. Your associates are of the most desperate character. They are as destructive as the lion of the forest. Oh! that I could induce you to forsake sin and become a useful member of society. Flee from it. Sin kills beyond the tomb. I trust you may reform and become the associate of Christians. If I forget to defend the holy institutions bequeathed to us by the Blessed Savior and His devoted followers, let my right hand forget its cunning.

We see the works of God and His power and glory in the starry sky. We see it in every blade of grass. We behold it in the great deep. May we, as a nation favored of God, keep His holy commandments and reverence the marriage vow. I admit there are causes which may justify separation. For instance: God, the Giver of our moral law, has declared in holy writ that adultery should be the only cause for a divorce; other causes may, in extreme cases, justify a separation; none of which operate in the present case. Persons often marry others who are not their equals, and who cannot be raised to their grade of intelligence. Such persons are placed in an unpleasant position. This alone should not justify a divorce, though mortifying to those who are connected with such persons. Incompatibility of temper is another evil that causes much unhappiness. Many other causes I could name, gentlemen of the jury, if time would permit. Let us reverence the God of our forefathers. He who directed the Pilgrim fathers in the days of darkness and despair. He nerved their souls when oppressed by British rule. When the sword, disease and hunger swept them down, the God of nations hovered around them. Their bloody foot-prints were left in the snow as an evidence of devotion to freedom and religious institutions. By His divine aid, they triumphed gloriously. Allow me to thank the court for its indulgence. I now, gentlemen of the jury, leave the case with you for your consideration, believing you think as I do that it is a conspiracy, formed for the overthrow of the great fabric of morality, and to crush the fond hopes and aspirations of the souls of those who cherish it.

CHAPTER VIII

At the closing of Mr. Montgomery's argument Judge Johnson charged the jury as follows:

Gentlemen of the Jury—This case is one that involves the interest of each of the parties to this suit. I regret much the unhappy results growing out of it. The marriage rite is a sacred one and should be preserved inviolate. We are told in sacred writ: "Those that God joined together, let no man put asunder." They become man and wife under those sacred vows. By their choice, they preferred their case to be tried by you, gentlemen of the jury, which is rather unusual, but it relieves me from the unpleasant duty of rendering a decision. Let me here say to you, gentlemen of the jury: First—Divest yourselves of all personal prejudices, if there should be any against either of the parties present. Second—Take into consideration the character of the witnesses here introduced for and against the parties interested in this suit, and their character for truth and veracity. Thirdly—Examine carefully the weight and bearing of said testimony given. Fourthly—Make a close analyzation of the facts and of the correspondence of Mrs. B. and Mr. Oldham. If then, in your judgment, you believe Mr. Brown, the defendant, to be guilty of the charges, it is for you to render a fair and impartial decision in favor of Mrs. B. If there should be any doubts on your minds, the defendant should have the benefit of said doubts. And if Mr. B. is not guilty, he should be honorably exonerated from the charges. The marriage rite must be respected, and the laws of our common country enforced to protect the weak against the encroachments of the strong.

The Judge then handed the letter to the foreman of the jury. The jurors retired, and after being out an hour and a half brought in a verdict of "not guilty," which was received by the spectators with loud applause.

The Judge then admonished them to bury the hatchet of domestic strife, and return to the embraces of each other. Mrs. B. advanced to her husband and threw her arms around his neck and kissed him, with tears rolling down her cheeks. The scene was truly indescribable, tears stood in every eye, and silence reigned throughout. This was an impressive lesson to them. They pledged themselves mutually that death alone should sever them from each other.

The Judge then addressed Aunt Polly, Martha Lovejoy and Mrs. H. as follows:

"I pity these unfortunate women who have taken pleasure in degrading themselves, and have sought to rob a virtuous lady of her character. The God of heaven has promised to be a husband to the Widow. His guarding angel has stood near her in this her hour of trial and affliction. Aunt Polly, Mrs. H. and Martha Lovejoy have sought for gold to blast the hope of the just, and to destroy the happiness of others, which gold nor silver cannot purchase. I have been on the bench for twenty years. I never witnessed such characters introduced in court. I regret much that an example cannot be made of such persons. Who is more to be feared than the slanderer? Who is more dangerous to society? God's revenge will visit them. You are guilty of the most heinous crime which is in the calendar, murder excepted. Your education has been neglected. You have become hardened in sin. I trust in God you never will enter this room while I occupy this bench."

The house resounded with applause. They stood trembling like prisoners condemned to death.

The Judge continued: "If I had the power, I would consign them to a prison that should be built and dedicated to slanderers and liars. No one is secure from their attacks. Every city, town and village is infested with such persons. They are a disgrace to any community. They are enemies to God and man. Who of us here have been exempt from the spleen of the calumniator, and our names heralded from house to house? Heaven is surely the only place exempt from the wicked. There the wicked cease from troubling, and the weary are forever at rest. Your verdict, gentlemen of the jury, gives me great satisfaction, and I trust the public generally will be benefited by it. Had these geniuses succeeded in their plans, so well arranged and conceived, the whole neighborhood would have been endangered. Every man and woman who felt the least aggrieved would apply for a bill, disregarding the holy rite of matrimony. We have established a precedent that heaven sanctions. I am proud to say Lawyer Montgomery has lifted high the banner of morality to-day. He has done his duty and done it well. If other counsellors would follow is example, we would soon have a far better state of things. For a paltry sum of money lawyers would divorce the Church of Christ, although purchased with His precious blood. Leave the Court, you vile wretches," said the Judge, to Aunt Polly and her disciples.

They were hooted out of the court, followed by an excited crowd. Many ladies gathered around the Widow and Mrs. B. Mr. B's friends congratulated him. Mrs. B. approached the Widow and fell upon her knees, with tears coursing down her cheeks and said:

"Will you forgive me? I have wronged truly my best and truest female companion."

The Widow kissed her and said:

"Nellie, I love you still."

They left the court-house together, Mrs. B. leaning upon her husband's arm, weeping as though her heart would break.

So ends the great divorce case of Virginia.

In conclusion, we have yet left many persons like Mrs. H., Aunt Polly, and Martha Lovejoy, whose chief delight is to meddle with everybody's business and sow the seeds of discord.

2. Octoroon Slave of Cuba

Jane Gray was the daughter of a wealthy physician of New Orleans. She possessed all the requirements of a finished education. She was handsome and charming. She swayed a magical influence over her associates. She moved in the first circles of society; she made many friends—none had less enemies. She was left an orphan at the tender age of one year and three months. Her father's brother adopted her. They spared neither money nor pains to educate her. Her father left her a handsome fortune at his death. Jane knew but little concerning her mother. She often heard Mrs. James Gray remark what a beautiful girl his sister Louisa was. How unfortunate it was she had been kidnapped. Jane never would have known that she had a sister, if it was not for the information derived from Mrs. Gray. She had many admirers. Gentlemen of refinement and wealth sought to capture her noble heart. These offers she declined. Through the course of social events she made the acquaintance of a Mr. Zevoe, a Cuban planter. He was by no means prepossessing or attractive, but he was reported to be worth two millions of dollars.

He was not long in securing her consent to unite with him in the sacred bonds of matrimony. Her adopted father and mother were not well pleased with her choice, but offered no serious objections. They regretted it much, because their blood had been kept pure so many generations with but a slight mixture of African blood coursing through Jane's veins (of which fact she was ignorant), should now be corrupted with Spanish mixture. However, they were married on the twenty-sixth day of September. Shortly after, they obtained passage on the old ship "Sea Monster," which was advertised to sail on the first day of October for Cuba. They made every preparation that was necessary for the voyage. On the morning of the first of October, at half-past eight o'clock, according to arrangement, a carriage was at the door of the residence. The morning was indeed lovely, and seemed to be the omen of happiness and joy to bride and groom. The two parlors were crowded with her friends and acquaintances, who came to bid her farewell. Many who could not gain access, rushed to the steamer to await their coming.

It was, indeed, a day long to be remembered. Women wept. Strong men with warm hearts could not conceal their tears. The bride and the groom entered the coach, accompanied by her adopted parents. The driver was not long in whirling them to the landing, where were congregated a host of her friends, who crowded aboard of the steamer to bid her an affectionate farewell. The captain, in the course of thirty minutes, gave orders to notify the guests to go ashore, which they did many with tears coursing down their cheeks. The signal was then given to cast off the moorings. Jane rushed on deck to gaze upon her friends ashore. By this time the steamer was drifting out in the deep and heading for the ocean. Jane Zevoe was so much affected, she could scarcely wave her handkerchief as a token of farewell. Jane lost sight of her friends in the distance. She then cast her weary eyes upon the stately domes and edifices of her native city. She looked eagerly upon them, until they faded from her view in the glorious sunlight of an Autumn day. Strange emotions filled her soul as the ocean widened the space between her and the home of her childhood. She retired to her state-room to reflect upon the scenes and pleasures of the past.

She wept long and bitterly. Her husband tried to soothe her grief by telling her to cast her all on him. To her he would be a father and a husband.

Nothing worthy of note transpired during the voyage. On the fifth day of October, the gallant ship cast anchor in the harbor of Havana. At half-past eight o'clock in the morning, Mr. and Mrs. Zevoe went ashore and ordered breakfast and a suite of rooms at the Planters' Hotel. Here they remained, recruiting themselves from the effects of their late voyage. Here she was the centre of attraction, and received many calls from the nobility of Cuba. She received the blessings of many who hoped that the radiant sunbeams of happiness and joy would shine brightly around her pathway.

On the twelfth day of October, her husband procured a carriage. They left early on that morning for his plantation, which was sixteen miles from the city of Havana. They arrived safe at four o'clock at their country mansion, which was not at all prepossessing to the bride for its architecture. Rachel, the negro servant, after shaking hands with her master, received a slight introduction to her new mistress, whom she escorted to the parlor, which looked cheerless and ancient to Mrs. Zevoe. The only furniture that it contained was a half dozen cane-bottom chairs, an old dingy desk, a settee, a rocking chair, and a plain old fashioned bureau. The floor was not robed with purple carpet, but was dressed with plain, common matting. Jane made herself as cheerful as circumstances would permit. She felt as though her brightest and happiest days had passed. Mr. Zevoe, after settling with the driver and arranging outside matters, entered the parlor.

He saw at a glance that she was neither cheerful nor happy. He engaged in conversation with her in regard to his future plans and prospects. While they were conversing, Rachel was busying herself preparing for supper. When the repast was ready she notified Mr. and Mrs. Zevoe. They entered the dining-room, which exhibited neither taste nor style. She partook of the supper, which did not suit her palate or appetite. After supper she concluded to take an observation of the rooms in the dwelling. Rachel, being delighted with her appearance, offered to escort her, which offer was accepted. They were not long in exploring the premises. She was more disappointed than she had been previously. They contained nothing worthy of note. She told Rachel she felt greatly disappointed in the appearance of things, but requested Rachel not to speak of it to her Master. She returned to the parlor unable to disguise her feelings.

He again renewed the conversation and asked her how she liked the appearance of things. She smiled, but not cheerfully, and said:

"I suppose it will do."

He then told her that he intended to furnish the house complete, and had left his order in New York, which he expected would arrive in thirty days. She thought it very strange that he did not have the house furnished previous to their arrival. He offered some slight excuse. The clock chimed ten, and they retired to bed. They arose next morning at eight and breakfasted, after which they took a morning walk. The air was pure, invigorating and fragrant with the odor of flowers. The sun was just climbing the eastern horizon, spreading its golden rays over Nature's favored landscape. The birds were pouring forth their melodies. All Nature seemed to lend its beauties and loveliness to welcome Jane Zevoe. Yet she was not happy. She told her husband of a strange dream she had during the night about her long lost sister. She saw her and conversed with her. He asked her under what circumstances she left.

"I only know what I learned from my adopted parents concerning Louisa," said Jane; "she was playing with some children in the neighborhood. She was not more than six or seven years of age at the time and was induced to follow a man under the promise of presenting her with candy and toys. She has never been seen from that day to this. They say they advertised for her in every paper in the State and offered large rewards for her recovery. That is all I know about it. I would give the world, with all its wealth, to see her. They tell me she is the striking likeness of my father."

"My dear, I sympathize with you. A sister's love is incomprehensible to one like myself. I have not a relative living on earth; but I will use my endeavors to assist you to recover her. I have a slave on this plantation that anybody would take to be you, not knowing that she had African blood in her veins."

"Ah, indeed," said Mrs. Zevoe; "I am sure she is not a relative of mine, for my family are of pure Saxon blood; nevertheless I would like to see her."

By this time they had returned to the house. He excused himself and left to attend to some business on the plantation. Mrs. Zevoe entered into conversation with Rachel and asked:

"Have you ever seen a colored woman on the plantation that your master says resembles me so much?"

"I have; she resembles you slightly."

"Where did you come from, Rachel?" asked Mrs. Zevoe.

"I came from New Orleans."

"Is it possible," says Mrs. Zevoe, "that you come from my native state? Tell me who you belonged to there?"

"I was owned when quite small, by a man named William Jackson. His property was attached for debt; myself and mother, including other slaves, were sold at public auction in New Orleans. A Doctor Gray purchased me to take care of a little girl called Jane, whose mother and an older sister the doctor sold, because she displeased him. He took a fancy to little Jane, and concluded to raise and educate her."

"Did you ever see the woman and child he sold?"

"No, madam; they were sold before I went to live with the doctor."

"How old do you think the girl was when she was sold?"

"I have heard others say she was between six and seven."

"How old was this child Jane, when you went to nurse her?"

"She was just able to toddle around a chair; indeed, I often felt sorry for the dear little creature, although I took great care of it. It ate and slept with me."

"How long did you live with the doctor?"

"Nine months."

"Why did you leave him?"

"He died during the nine months. His brother was left executor of the doctor's estate; they concluded to adopt little Jane as their own child. The doctor's brother was opposed to holding slaves; he sold me to a minister, who promised to take good care of me. I went to live with him; his wife's health was very poor. They concluded to take a trip to Cuba to improve her health. We arrived here safe. I waited upon her day and night; by constant care and attention a change took place for the better, and in six months she finally recovered. For my faithful attention to her, they promised never to part with me. After remaining here eight months, they concluded again to return to Louisiana. The day before they left I was notified, by a gentleman, that I was his individual property. This I could not believe; I rushed into the sitting-room, where my mistress was, and asked her if such were the facts. She replied:

"'Rachel, our means are about exhausted. Mr. Cook was compelled to dispose of you to raise funds, as he did not wish to send home for more means. I think, Rachel, you have a good master in Mr. Zevoe, and a comfortable home, so you must endeavor to make yourself contented.' Tears coursed down my cheeks as those words fell from her lips. I long entertained the hope of returning home with them."

"Indeed, they treated you very mean. But you must put your trust in God. His blessings and His mercies He bestows upon the just and the good. His vengeance and His wrath shall visit the unjust. I shall do all in my power to make matters pleasant for you during my stay."

Rachel thanked her kindly.

The following morning Mrs. Zevoe and Rachel prepared themselves to call and see Louisa. Rachel remarked before leaving the house:

"Mr. Zevoe would not like it, as he notified me to have no communication with her whatever, and I have not seen her but once since I have been here."

"What does she do, Rachel?"

"I don't think she does anything more than take care of her house and children when they are at home."

"Is not her children with her?"

"No, madam; Mr. Zevoe wrote from New Orleans before he started, to have the children moved to the Lower Plantation, which orders were complied with."

"Who is the father of her children?"

Rachel smiled, and said:

"Indeed, I could not say."

"Whether it pleases or displeases Mr. Zevoe, we shall call to see her. What is the distance from here to her house?"

"Three miles."

"It will be a pleasant walk for us."

They started and by half-past nine o'clock stood in front of a neat cabin, covered with honey-suckles. They knocked. The door was opened by a woman who was fairer than her master, prepossessing in her appearance and affable. Rachel remarked to Louise:

"I wish to introduce you to our new mistress, Mrs. Zevoe."

Here stood the handmaid of slavery and the queen of refinement. Louisa acknowledged her superiority with a polite bow. Mrs. Zevoe saw at a glance a striking resemblance between Louisa and her father's portrait, which hung in the parlors of her adopted parents. They entered into conversation, during which Mrs. Zevoe asked Louisa where she was from. She answered:

"I was born in the city of New Orleans."

"When did you leave there?"

"I suppose it is now about eighteen years."

"Under what circumstances did you leave?"

"My mother and I were sold to a planter in Texas, by the name of Cravan. He promised not to separate us. After living with him one year, he sold me to a man by the name of Hood, whom I must say had neither principle nor honor. I declared I would not live with him. He sold me to Mr. Zevoe, the father of your husband."

"How long have you been here?"

"Nearly ten years."

"Are you married?"

"I am not, although the mother of three children."

"Pray tell me who is the father of your children?"

Louisa hesitated a few moments and said:

"It is not for me to say; you will know, perhaps, if you remain on the plantation."

Mrs. Zevoe could scarcely suppress her love and affection for Louisa. She believed her to be her long-lost sister. She asked:

"I suppose you have some knowledge of your mother?"

"I have; I often see her tall form and her cheerful countenance in my mind."

"Was she handsome?"

"She was not; but she had one of the sweetest dispositions that a woman was ever blessed with."

"What was her complexion?"

"She was a brown-copper color, with long wavy hair and good features."

"Had she any other children besides yourself?"

"She had a baby called Jane, of which I have a faint recollection."

Louisa and Rachel both noticed that Mrs. Zevoe labored under great mental embarrassment which she was endeavoring to overcome. Louisa and Rachel were intelligent and might be regarded as judges of human nature. They knew not what wrought upon her feelings, unless she believed that Mr. Zevoe was the father of Louisa's children.

"Louisa," said Mrs. Zevoe, "I pity your condition."

Here again, her feelings showed signs of distress.

"I may be of service to you. If I can possibly better your condition, I shall use my best endeavors to do so."

She bade her good-bye, and promised to see her at an early day. She was convinced Louisa was her sister, and that Rachel had watched over her when [she was] a little infant; but she revealed the secret to neither of them. She remarked to Rachel on their return:

"I want you to tell me, confidentially, what you think of Mr. Zevoe. I have, in a degree, lost confidence in the man. I believe he gambles. My reasons for thinking so is—he sat up two nights on our voyage and came in to the state-room several times to get sums of money. Besides I have detected him in several stories."

"If I can speak with you confidentially, I will post you a little," replied Rachel.

"You can place implicit confidence in me. I will never divulge a word of it."

"I am sorry for you; I know him well. He is not the man to make you happy. I am expecting every day to see every thing on this plantation attached for debt, myself included."

"Can it be possible?"

"Yes; it is mortgaged for every dollar it is worth."

"Oh, heavens! What silly creatures women are to be duped by such men. But say nothing. I will endeavor by stratagem to secure your freedom. Do you believe he left his orders in New York for furniture to be shipped?"

Rachel shook her head, and said:

"You don't know the man."

"I have made up my mind firmly to make my stay here but short. Has he anything?"

"He has a small plantation south of here, which I believe is not mortgaged. The overseer claims it in order to keep off his creditors. It is said to be worth thirty or forty thousand dollars."

"If such is the fact, I shall try to revenge myself upon him."

When they returned home, Mr. Zevoe was there. He had been absent nearly the entire day. Mrs. Zevoe approached him affectionately and kissed him. He said:

"Dear Jane, I could not live without your presence."

"I am happy to know that you love me, and love me dearly," replied Mrs. Zevoe.

"Have you been taking a walk?"

"I called to see your white slave."

"I am surprised at your thinking that she is white."

He continued the conversation by asking her what she thought of Louisa.

Mrs. Zevoe carelessly remarked:

"I think she would make me a good waiting-maid. With her and Rachel, I think I could run this establishment, and make myself contented. I have one request to make of you."

"What is it, my dear?"

"I want you to make me out a bill of sale in my own name for Louisa and Rachel, making them my own individual property."

Mr. Zevoe laughed and said:

"That is just what I intended doing."

"Louisa has three children, has she not?"

He seemed for a moment silent. After recovering himself, he replied:

"She has."

"Who is the father of her children?"

"That is a matter I have not troubled myself to ascertain. We are glad to have our property increase. It pays good interest on the money invested."

Mrs. Zevoe smiled, and said:

"You will not think I am at all inquisitive. It is a matter that interests me but little."

"To-morrow I will get Lawyer Wilson to draw up the papers. He will be in the neighborhood, and he promised to make me a call before returning."

Accordingly, the lawyer arrived the following morning. Mr. Zevoe was not in at the time. The madam and [he] entered into conversation. She informed him what she desired him to do. Lawyer Wilson asked her if she had the consent of her husband, and if he would sign the papers. Mrs. Zevoe said he would. He then said:

"It will be a capital thing for you. I have been his attorney for years."

"How does his business matters stand?"

"They are not in a healthy condition. I shall advise him also to make over the Lower Plantation to you."

"I hope you will. I think you have influence enough with him to affect it."

During the conversation, Mr. Zevoe made his appearance and expressed himself highly gratified to see Lawyer Wilson. After conversing a few moments, he told the counsellor what he desired him to do in reference to Rachel and Louisa.

"It is a wise act upon your part."

The lawyer asked him to step outside; he wished to have a private conversation with him. They walked out and had quite a consultation. His attorney said:

"Your affairs are in a critical condition. The mortgage on your property will be due in a few days. I am satisfied you are not in a condition to meet it. If so, you had better give your wife a deed also of the Lower Plantation."

"You are aware that my overseer, Mr. Lamar, has a deed of that property.

"I am satisfied he will cancel it if agreeable to you."

"Perfectly."

"Where is he?"

"He left here a short time since for Havana on business; he will not return for several days."

"I will see him in the city and have a talk with him about it."

They then returned to the house and took the names of Louisa and Rachel, and their ages.

"The documents will be prepared day after to-morrow. You must sign them, and I will have them recorded," said Lawyer Wilson.

"I shall be in town in a day or two, and will call at your office."

After dining, the lawyer bade them good day. The following day he met Mr. Lamar in the streets of Havana and spoke to him on the subject. He said he was perfectly willing to resign his claims to the plantation, notwithstanding Mr. Zevoe owed him some twelve hundred dollars; yet he had confidence that Mr. Zevoe would pay every dollar. Lawyer Wilson took him to the Recorder's office to cancel his claim, with the understanding that Mr. Zevoe would give him his note, with an endorser for the amount. The lawyer gave him his word that it would be done, and made out the papers, turning the estate, together with Louisa and her children and Rachel, over to Mrs. Zevoe. The second day following, Mr. Zevoe arrived in the city. The documents were signed and recorded.

Mr. Zevoe told Lawyer Wilson that his wife wished him to call out and see her in the course of a few days. He said he would go and bring the documents with him. Owing to a pressure of business he was detained. He wrote her a letter congratulating her on her success—telling her he would call and see her as soon as an opportunity would afford. She wrote a reply asking him to make out free papers for Rachel and Louisa and her children, and to bring them when he came, but not to divulge it to any living soul.

Mr. Zevoe was absent some days before returning. During this time, Mrs. Zevoe again called upon Louisa and said:

"Louisa, the lost is found."

"What have you lost and found?"

"I lost a beloved sister years ago."

She threw her arms around her neck, embraced and kissed her, and said:

"You are my beloved sister."

"Oh, heavens!" exclaimed Louisa, "can it be that this is my dear sister Jane?"

Mrs. Zevoe was overcome and could not utter a sentence. When she recovered, she said:

"This is Jane. Oh! how I have longed to see you. But much to my surprise and shame, I find you the victim of slavery and the concubine of your own master, who regards you and your children as *chattels.* What a cursed institution slavery is! How damning is its effects! It fetters the intellect and robs virtue of its purest jewel. It brings shame and disgrace to the door of many a woman who would be an ornament to society, were it not for the cursed sin. Though a woman's skin be black, her soul can be as pure as the purest Saxon. I have been reared in the lap of luxury. I am the favored child of fortune."

"Can you not redeem me from this life of shame and degradation?" asked Louisa.

"I will free you and your children at all hazards."

They again embraced each other and wept. Jane said:

"You shall be as free as the air that blows. I desire you to keep this a secret to the grave. Do not reveal that I am the daughter of a Negro woman or the sister of a slave. It would blast my hopes forever in this life. It would leave a stain upon me that never could be wiped out. You know the prejudices that are entertained against persons in whose veins course the slightest mixture of African blood. I have moved in the first circles of society and have been the guest of the wealthiest families of my State. I was educated to believe I was of the purest Saxon blood. How humiliating it would be to me to be rejected and scorned because of my origin. I myself entertain no prejudices against caste, and acknowledge God to be the common father of the human family. But, Louisa, be cheerful. I will be your benefactor."

She bade Louisa good-bye and requested her to call and bring the children to the house on the following Thursday. She then left for home. When she arrived Rachel told her that Lawyer Wilson had called and left a package for her, and that he regretted her absence."

"I should have liked so much to have seen him," said Mrs. Zevoe.

She took a seat and opened the package. It contained the documents making Rachel, Louisa and her children, and the Lower Plantation, her individual property. She felt much delighted, but did not mention it to Rachel. Mr. Zevoe returned from Havana the following morning. He did not find Mrs. Zevoe as cheerful as he expected. He told her what he had done in making her the sole owner of certain property. She thanked him and asked if the plantation on which they lived was free from debt. He said it was.

"I heard in Havana that your home plantation was mortgaged for every dollar it was worth," said Mrs. Zevoe.

"Nonsense; you know there are persons in this world who attend to everybody's business but their own. Such characters, my dear, envy you your wealth."

Little did he think that she knew the depth of his purse and the amount of his liabilities. He supposed he had a young woman that would give herself more concern about social pleasures than business matters. But such was not the case. Mr. Zevoe, after they had quite a chat, asked her if she would not loan him fifteen hundred dollars as he had a speculation in view which would pay him well for the amount invested.

"You are aware that you have already used some twenty-five hundred dollars of my money."

"I am; I will have a check from New York in a few days for ten thousand dollars. Then I will return you the amount."

"As you are expecting it in a few days, you had better not make any investment until you receive it."

Mrs. Zevoe winked at Rachel and smiled. Mr. Zevoe left the house. Mrs. Zevoe laughed, and remarked to Rachel:

"I judge he takes me to be an unsophisticated wife."

"I think so too."

"Rachel, you will see a change here on Thursday next."

"Do you intend leaving us so soon?"

"You will know when the time comes."

Rachel was totally ignorant of what Mrs. Zevoe had in contemplation, or of the relationship existing between Louisa and Mrs. Zevoe.

"I trust you will never leave me here," said Rachel.

"Keep a good heart. Be hopeful. God works in mysterious ways, His wonders to perform."

"That is true. I have been a believer in His goodness and His mercy for a number of years."

"Still trust in Him," said Mrs. Zevoe.

Mr. Zevoe returned to the house, but did not seem to be in very good humor.

Nothing special transpired until Thursday morning, when Louisa arrived with her children. Mr. Zevoe was the first person Louisa met when she approached the house. He remarked:

"How do you do, Louisa? I suppose you have called to make your mistress a visit."

She smiled. He then spoke to her in a tone not audible. Rachel was busying herself about the kitchen, yet she had an eye on her master and Louisa. Mr. Z. requested her to go in the kitchen and take a seat and he would notify her mistress of her arrival. He walked into the parlor and told Mrs. Zevoe that her maid had come.

"Who?" she asked.

"Louisa and her brats."

"Ask her to walk in the parlor."

On her entering the parlor, neither Jane nor Louisa betrayed any signs of friendship. Mrs. Zevoe remarked to Louisa:

"Are those your children?"

"Yes," replied Louisa.

"They are fine and healthy looking."

Mr. Zevoe sat without taking any part in the conversation. It was the first time that Mrs. Zevoe had seen Louisa's children. After learning the names of the children, she took little Eddy by the hand and said in an excited tone:

"Mr. Zevoe, I have the painful duty of introducing you to your own children. They are bone of your bone, flesh of your flesh."

He started from his seat, saying:

"Madam, I deny the charge."

Mrs. Zevoe, pointing to little Eddy, said:

"That child alone is sufficient evidence to convict you of the charge in any Court; he is, indeed, a photograph of the man who disowns his own children, that a king would be proud of."

"Your brain, madam, must be diseased."

"Louisa, upon this issue is hinged your freedom and future happiness. I ask you a question to-day that I never asked you before. Are not these children Charles Zevoe's?"

Louisa hung her head and blushed.

"I wish you to tell me the whole truth," said Mrs. Zevoe.

Louisa, in a tremulous voice, said:

"They are."

Mr. Zevoe rushed towards Louisa like a madman. Jane stepped between them, as fearless as a Roman soldier, and defied him to lay his hands upon her at the peril of his life, and exclaimed:

"I have sworn this day, in the presence of high heaven, never to live with you again. I have decreed my own divorce. She, sir, was as pure as the fleeting snow until you robbed her of chastity and liberty. If you possessed a spark of manhood, you would love her and honor her children. You regard her as your inferior, because a tinge of African blood courses through her veins. She is too noble a creature to be your slave or your wife."

Under that roof, slavery and freedom met hope and despair. Joy and sorrow each struggled to defend freedom's claims. Jane, armed with the weapons of Justice and Truth, struck slavery a terrible blow. Her soul was inflamed, her feelings aroused and her pride wounded, to find her sister the subject of slavery.

Jane continued:

"It is to her, sir, you owe your love and affection. She has borne you three lovely children."

Louisa was much affected; Rachel stood by with tears in her eyes. Mr. Zevoe remained silent. His very soul wrung with bitterness. She took Louisa by the hand and led her affectionately to where he was seated.

"Charles Zevoe, I ask you to-day—will you not accept of Louisa to be your wedded wife. My name is no longer Jane Zevoe, but Jane Gray."

He spoke not a sentence. Mrs. Zevoe said:

"Louisa, by power in me invested, I install you mistress of this castle. Here are papers securing to you and your children freedom. I will also make you a deed to the Lower Plantation. I will secure Lawyer Wilson to see that you are protected in your liberty and property. God forbid! I should reap the benefits of that which justly belongs to you and your children. Be careful and do not allow yourself to be swindled out of the property I shall deed to you. I stand here to-day as a minister of justice and the advocate of human rights. I ask you, Charles Zevoe, in the presence of high heaven, will you not take Louisa to be your wife? Treat her as a companion, not as a slave. Your silence, I suppose, gives consent."

She then placed her hand in his. Lifting her eyes heavenward, [she] offered a fervent and devout prayer, and pronounced them man and wife. She kissed each of them and blessed the children. She then said to Louisa:

"I wish to speak with you privately."

They entered the adjoining room. She said:

"To-morrow morning I shall bid you farewell!"

Neither could subdue their feelings.

"Dear sister," said Louisa, "do you intend to leave me? What will become of me?"

"I am ever your sister in the bonds of affection; you must write me often—under an assumed name. I expect a carriage to arrive here every moment. If it arrives we shall be off to-morrow morning, bright and early."

"Do you intend to take Rachel with you?"

"Yes, poor thing. I could not think of leaving her behind. She will be the only recompense I will have for the twenty-five hundred dollars that Mr. Zevoe used of my money. I have her free papers in my possession and will give them to her when we arrive in New Orleans."

On her return to the room she said:

"Charles Zevoe, I freely forgive you for the injuries I received at your hands. I will not expose you. My parting request is to treat Louisa as becomes a husband. Educate your children and respect her. I will wear the weeds of mourning for you when I return to that home where the sunshine of gladness, joy and peace ever shed its effulgent rays. No night of gloom or sadness entered its chambers. If you are asked for I will tell my friends I have buried you in the sea of forgetfulness. However unpleasant it may be, circumstances compel me to pursue this course. However sacred the bonds of matrimony may be regarded, I look upon it as being a civil contract between the parties, and when either wilfully and knowingly violate its duties, I hold it to be the duty of the injured party to seek redress. There is no law, temporal or Divine, that can compel a woman or a man to live with those who are repugnant to them. It behooves every individual to seek happiness, regardless of the smiles and frowns of the world. Personal pride induce many to eke out a miserable existence, who have married persons not adapted to them in feeling or disposition. I, this day, decree my own divorce. Whether censured or sustained by public sentiment—I care not. Honesty, virtue, truth and diligence cling together and hang around the neck of memory."

"Can it be that you had discarded my affections, deceived and betrayed my confidence?" asked Mr. Zevoe.

"I look not to the fleeting shadows of time, but to eternity. Where the secrets of all hearts shall be revealed. If I have done good, I shall be the recipient of the mercies of a just God. If wrong, even in this case, I shall receive His condemnation. Conscience, sir, like a thorn, is ever pricking the soul of the wicked, warning them to repent. It is the faithful sentinel of God. I wish you not to entertain the slightest hopes of me. I am dead to you—dead forever! I intend again to launch this frail bark upon the ocean of chance, never, I hope, to be captured by a pirate in disguise!"

"Do you consider me to be a pirate?" asked he.

"I do; one of the deepest dye."

"What have I robbed you of?"

"Of my good name and my happiness."

Mr. Zevoe stood like a prisoner, condemned without hope.

"Shall crime, guilt and sin outlive Justice, Truth, and Righteousness. No! never! My soul was sick within me when I entered this castle. It bore the signs of misery, distress and unhappiness. I have, sir, one request to ask of you. Will you treat Louisa as your bosom companion?"

About seven o'clock P.M., the coach arrived; they intended starting early the following morning. Miss Jane and Rachel prepared themselves for the trip. Rachel was greatly overjoyed when Miss Jane informed her that she intended taking her to New Orleans. She charged Rachel, on her arrival home, never to speak of the circumstances. If she did, to say Charles Zevoe was dead. Rachel promised to do as requested.

Mr. Zevoe and Rachel are still ignorant of the relationship of Jane to Louisa.

Nothing occurred during the evening. After supper, the new bride and her children occupied the room of the late Mrs. Zevoe. Miss Gray and Rachel slept together. Strange to say, she arose with a complexion as fair as ever after sleeping with a Negro woman. They bade Louisa an affectionate farewell, and kissed the children. Mr. Zevoe was so much enraged that he left the house before breakfast and did not return.

The parting scene was truly affecting. Jane promised Louisa, faithfully, she would write on her arrival at New Orleans. They stepped into the carriage and bade Mr. Zevoe and his plantation a final adieu.

3. My Trip to Baltimore

I once lived in the District of Columbia, near the National capitol. I had a friend who resided in Bladensburg, about six miles from the City of Washington, named William Savoy. He was a white nigger. I had occasion to go to Baltimore. I concluded to make my friend a visit, as Bladensburg lay directly on the turnpike. About this time the stage coaches were transmogrified into railroad cars, and horses manufactured into steam engines. That, you know, added greatly to their speed. In accordance with my plans, I visited my friend William. He was delighted to see me, and made me agreeably welcome, notwithstanding he was much whiter than myself. He cooked for himself. Opposite to him lived a white family, from whom he bought milk. The morning after I arrived, the rain poured down in torrents. He asked me to go over and get some milk while he prepared breakfast, which I did. I knocked at the milk-lady's door hastily; having a desire to get shelter from the rain. She opened the door. I presented my milk pitcher. She received it with one hand and closed the door in my face. Of course I said nothing. I had learned even in that dark age of the world that many whites disliked the nigger—some for one thing, some for another. In most cases, because of his color.

Next morning, my friend William went over for milk. He knocked and was invited in. He stayed so long I finally went to look for him. I knocked at the door. The landlady opened it and there sat William at the breakfast table with the white folks. The lady ordered me around to the kitchen door, which I readily obeyed. After reflecting, I said: "Well, well! the whiter the Nigger the better he is, and the nearer he is a man." I began to think how fortunate he was to have white blood in his veins, although he was not entirely free from suspicion. The Negro, as usual, stuck out in his hair. It would not require a microscope to detect it. One would have to understand Negro physiology well to notice it. The landlady asked my friend where I was from. He told her from Washington. She asked him if I was a free Negro. To carry the joke out, he told her that I belonged to his father.

The next day, the landlady called me over and cordially invited me in, which I thought very strange from the previous reception I had received. This, I found out, was on account of my belonging to William's father. She asked me many questions. Among others, if his family was wealthy. I answered in the affirmative. She then asked me what he was. "Why," said I, "he is a man." "No," she said, "I don't mean that. Is he an American?" I said: "Madam, he is part Moligascar, part English, part French, and part Irish." "Why, dear me!" said she, "how can that be?" "Well," said I, "Madam, it takes a good many ingredients to make a man." "That's so," she said. "It has been whispered around here that he had Negro blood in him." "No, Madam," said I. "I am glad to hear it," said she, "I can stand anything but that. He is a nice gentleman, is he not?" Of course I said "Yes," without reflecting that he was a Nigger.

I concluded to be half white was an advantage, and I desired to get amalgamated, if possible. I asked my friend where that family was from. He said New York. We had a hearty laugh over it.

The next morning I parted with him, and did not betray his secret, which added greatly to his success. I started on my journey about noon. The same day I rode up to a hotel for dinner, kept by one Henry Weston. He was seated on the porch. I asked him if I could get dinner and have my horse fed. "Certainly," he replied, and he called the hostler to take care of my horse. I saw at a glance that he was a gentleman.

The servant-woman was not long in preparing dinner, as there were several others waiting. In a few minutes, the dinner-bell rang. I did not rush in with the others. He came out and told me to walk in the dining-room and get dinner. I entered and found a table spread with the very best to sustain the inner-man. After dinner, he passed cigars around, myself not excluded.

I was wonderfully struck at receiving such treatment. I then asked him for my bill. "Not a cent," said he. "Well! well!" said I to myself, "how is this?" I thanked him kindly. He ordered my horse to be brought up, and in a little while the hostler had him at the door. I put a dollar in his hand. He thanked me a dozen times. I then had the curiosity to know where this gentleman was raised. He told me in Maryland. I bade him good day, and started off.

The next house I made was about dark. I saw a man unhitching a horse from a buggy. I spoke to him as politely as I knew how, and he did not even as much as look at me. I asked him if I could get supper and shelter for my horse for the night. He said, very grumly: "Take him to the barn—give him a gallon of oats, and go around to the kitchen and ask my wife for supper." His order I obeyed of course. I attributed the indifference with which he treated me owing to my not being half white. I then determined, if possible, to get amalgamated, thinking it would be of great advantage to me. I entered the kitchen, spoke to the lady and told her that I wished supper. She scarcely grunted when I spoke to her, and, while preparing the supper, she seemed to eye me with jealousy. I felt very uncomfortably situated. The supper was soon prepared and placed upon a table, which looked as though it had neither water or soap applied to it for a year.

By the time I got through supper, her husband came in. He asked me where I was from, and where I was going. During all this time, the landlady had not spoken a half dozen words to me. I told him that I was from Washington, and on my way to Baltimore. I then asked him a few questions, which he answered very readily. His wife asked me if there were many Negroes in Washington. I told her there were a good many. She remarked where she came from, there were very few, and they were the biggest thieves that ever lived. I asked her where she was from. She said the State of Indiana.

I concluded that the treatment I had received was not owing to my being black, but it was on account of those thieving Negroes in Indiana. I then said: "Madam, there are exceptions. All Negroes are not alike." She replied: "I never saw one that was worth his salt, or had the energy and enterprise to conduct any business, except one, and he soon played himself out." I asked her how that was. She said: "He was a middling fair scholar, lived in good style and dressed well. Consequently, the whites decided not to patronize him." I said: "Madam, it is difficult for colored men to succeed in business, especially in communities where they have 'Nigger on the brain,' unless he is humble in the extreme, and has a grin for everybody. With many, he must forget that he is a man, to succeed." She said: "I don't think it; if Negroes behave themselves they will be sustained." I said: "Madam, that rule don't always work. Did this man, of whom you just speak, misbehave? Was he disposed to be discourteous to his friends and patrons?" She said: "No; he did not; but some thought he was inclined to feel rather pompous; for this reason, they declined to patronize him. Where I came from, you know, if one gets down on a Nigger they all go against him." I told her it was very different where I came from, if a colored man was honest and upright, he invariably found friends who were willing to aid and assist him in business. After all, I concluded that she did not understand as much about the ingredients the Negro is composed of as the milk-woman at Bladensburg.

Feeling rather uncomfortable I expressed a wish to retire. I was shown to a loft over the kitchen and had to ascend it by a ladder. It looked more like a chicken roost than anything else I could compare it to. The bed contained about as much straw as would make a hen's nest, without sheets or pillows. Of course, I slept a little during the night, and studied how I should get even for the treatment I had received. I decided to get up early in the morning. Which I did, taking with me from the bed one of the best blankets, put it under my saddle, and gave my horse all the oats he could eat. I then ate all that I could possibly contain.

This was the only redress I could get. I paid my bill and by three o'clock that afternoon arrived in Baltimore City, and was again free from those perplexities so common to colored men. And I trust that if they are yet living they have a better opinion of Negro honesty. Should they again come in contact with Negroes, I hope they will treat them better.

4. Central Pacific Railroad

We are, perhaps, justified in speaking of the great achievement of the age—the Pacific Railroad—its undertaking and completion—the adverse and trying circumstances. Its success is due to ex-Governor Stanford, ——— Hopkins, Charles Crocker, combined with the united efforts of many people of the Pacific Coast and the Congress of the United States. Many regarded the project to be an impossibility. Those noble fathers of the enterprise despaired not, though often pressed to extremes for means. Perplexed with difficulties on every side, they went forward making the hilly ways level and the rough smooth. They split the rugged mountains, lifted the watery valleys, and opened a highway that had been closed since creation's morn until victory crowned their success. The iron horse can be seen darting to and fro with lightning speed, defying the mountain giants to check its onward course. A wonderful enterprise! Glorious results will emanate from the bands that hold California and the Atlantic States in their iron grasp. The emigration induced by quick transportation to this coast will be of great advantage to California. She must seek to hold her own against Eastern trade, and cope in every pursuit of industry. Her agricultural lands, her new and rising manufactories, her hardy and enterprising citizens, unite to make her still the Queen of the States in this Union.

"Honor to whom honor is due."

Of Elko, I shall not say much for or against, as a nobleman once said about America. I use the same language in reference to Elko. "She is a giantess without bones." The time may come when she will be classed among the leading cities of this State. There is a wonderful scope left for improvement. In speaking of her citizens, they are not excelled by any class on this coast.

5. Idaho City, Its Customs and Future Prospects

Idaho City is a noted mountain town, situated in a basin. Its citizens are liberal and generous. The mines are inexhaustible. The future prospects of the city are flattering. We expect it to become the terminus of every railroad in the Territory as well as the emporium of the North. Why the Territorial Fathers don't introduce gas-lights in the city is really astonishing. Property is advancing in value daily. The lumbermen are the chief benefactors of the city. Conflagrations lay it waste about once a year. We can stand it! Every property-holder is able to rebuild and meet his demands promptly. They seldom allow a bill to be presented the second time. The pioneers of the country have amassed large fortunes and retired from business. Merchants keep up the old customs of former days. They never fail to present their bill on Monday morning with a pleasant smile. If not paid, their countenances change. Miners are exceptions. They are all honorable, and will have plenty of cash when the birds sing and the waters run. Clerks, by strict economy, may soon be able to buy out their employers. Saloon keepers do an extensive business, especially in the Winter. They have lots of stove customers, who seldom make room for others, or spend a dime. It don't cost anything to run a saloon in the Winter! Butchers and bakers know not the want of money. Your patronage is solicited by all business men if you have cash and ask no credit!

We have an institution called the "Cold-water Tank." All of 'em are joining it, 'cept de Niggers; they can fill their kegs until it runs out of their eyes. They are of no use to the community, and the sooner whiskey kills 'em, the better.

Barbers are a fine set of fellows; they never condescend to speak disparagingly of each other. They are all finished workmen, and have received the Tonsorial Diploma. Some of them are a little selfish, and claim to do better work than any one else, and of course they know it all, because they have had a better opportunity of receiving a finished education than some others; consequently they are better than others and are ready to condemn their efforts, but do but little themselves.

6. Progress of America

This nation is one of the greatest that inhabits the globe. Her growth has been rapid. Indeed, she is a mammoth for her age. In science and literature she is not excelled. Her commerce whitens every sea. Her forts look out from every available point. Her sentinels, with glittering bayonets guard well her interests. Her territories are boundless in extent. Her fertile valleys invite the industrious husbandman to become her companion. Her minerals are inexhaustible and [illmitable]. The iron horse darts through every productive valley, breathing fire at every revolution. Her wildernesses, which were the abode of wild beasts and the Indian's wigwam, have now become large and populous cities. Civilization is spreading her benign influence far and wide. The heathen worship at her altars, and exclaim: "Wonderful are thy beauties." Our steamboats and crafts float upon every navigable stream. The finny tribe sport in countless thousands in our rivers, lakes and seas. Our statesmen are learned and sagacious. Our iron-clads are almost as impregnable as the Rocks of Gibraltar: our navy is not equaled for improved weapons of war. This government is advancing, step by step, to the grandeur and glory of greatness.

The spirit of the heroes of 1776 is still kept alive. The words of the immortal Patrick Henry will live until this great nation is extinct. When preparing a crusade against British tyranny, he said: "Give me liberty or give me death."

May this Republic forever be "the land of the free and the home of the brave."

The immortal Washington wrote his fame upon the great ledger of time with his sword in that memorable struggle.

The hero of the battle of New Orleans still lives in the hearts of his countrymen. He was a statesman, a soldier and a patriot, and died in the arms of the nation.

Crispus Attucks,* the first who offered his life a sacrifice to American liberty, is numbered among the heroes of 1776.

The teachings of that great and good man, Daniel O'Connell—a British subject—upon the altar of whose heart the fires of liberty burned, advocated the freedom of all men, regardless of nationality, creed or color.

---

*Crispus Attucks, a colored man, was the first that fell upon the plains of Boston, in the battle of April 5th, 1770.

7. Boise City

We shall not attempt to give a graphic description of the place. It is a neat little burg, situated in a beautiful and fertile valley, and is the capital of Idaho Territory. It contains many permanent buildings, including neat and handsome cottages. It being a central point, it has many advantages over its sister towns. It contains a population ranging from nine to twelve hundred inhabitants. Many of its citizens are afflicted with the terrible disease of Negrophobia. The very air seems to be pregnated with this disease. A respectable colored man can scarcely get accommodations at any of the hotels or restaurants. I was compelled, on my way from Idaho City to Silver City, to lay over from five P.M. until two A.M. the following morning. A few moments before the stage started for Silver City, I was invited by a swarthy, but generous-looking Spaniard, to take a cigar. We started down the street. The most of the saloons at this unseasonable hour being closed, my companion saw a light in a saloon kept by Mr. J. Old. We entered and called for what we wanted. The polite and accommodating Mr. Old bent over the counter and said, in a low tone of voice: "Detter, I cannot accommodate you." I regarded it as a polite insult, and walked out. He was the last man I expected that would treat me thus. Had I approached him with my hat in my hand, trembling like a quarry slave, I have no doubt this proud Saxon would have accommodated me. I have seen many like Mr. Old come to naught, and who would gladly accept a favor, though extended by a Negro. I have lived in mountain towns where the lowest and basest females, white and colored, could be served with meals. If a respectable colored man desired a meal, the landlord would politely invite him to be seated in the kitchen. I ever have and ever will take issue against any such treatment. In my travels wherever I have met gentlemen, they have always treated me as a man, and not as a thing. The rough usages and insults that colored men receive, invariably come from that class of whites who have little to recommend them outside of a white skin. Were I to say that there are no good feeling men in Boise City, I would be doing an injustice, to many. I appreciate my friends. I never can condescend to lick the hand that smites me, nor respect the man that insults me.

8. Give the Negro a Chance

The white man still clings to his prejudices against the colored race. It is difficult for a Negro to hire a pew in a church where the white Christian worships, however respectable he may be. They never crowd you in cars if they notice your skin is dark. None are considered ladies or gentlemen through whose veins flow African blood. Such are the prejudices and education of many Americans. I remember, when traveling between this city and Sacramento, colored people, however genteel, were compelled to share the deck with the horned cattle. A colored man travelling by stage, was compelled to wait until every passenger was aboard. If there was no room inside, he was ordered to the top or in the boot, as live baggage. How often the Negro has been hunted down in the broad sunlight of day, assassinated and murdered, and the assassin permitted to go unpunished, because his victim was as powerless as he was innocent. Having no rights a white was compelled to respect, even in the free State of California, [so] strong was the prevailing element. We have lived to see a higher state of civilization, and rejoice in its progress. We love the land that gave us birth, and all we ask of the white man is to give us an even chance in the great race of life. If you need a man to perform labor, and the Negro is competent and trustworthy, give him work. Don't deny him his bread, because he has a dark skin. Give him the same wages you give the white man. We are natives of the soil. We were with you when the corner-stone of this Republic was laid. We claim your consideration and aid. Close not against us the door of industry.

Help us to rise from the pit of degradation. Help us to go forward in the pathway that leads to grandeur and greatness. Our race have given their life-blood in every struggle this country has had, and have fallen side by side with the Saxon: White men! Conquer your prejudices.

9. Uncle Joe

In the County of Anne Arundel resided an old Negro who had laid down the shovel and the hoe. He belonged to Samuel Bell, a large planter. His name was Joe. He said his legs refused to discharge their duty; consequently, he could not walk. He was left in charge of the Negro quarters. His comrades became suspicious of his sincerity with reference to his lameness. They concluded to see if there was any virtue in his legs.

The Negroes on the adjoining plantation gave a party, as was customary among plantation Negroes, every Saturday evening. Joe was among the invited guests. He said: "You know I'd like to go dar, childens, but I can't walk." Two of his associates agreed to pack him by turns. He readily accepted their generous proposition. They went out and held a consultation. After a while they finally agreed upon a plan, that an individual should be placed at the graveyard on their return to act the ghost. They went to the entertainment and packed Uncle Joe. When the exercises of the evening closed, they shouldered Uncle Joe, and started for home. Joe seemed highly delighted with the evening's pleasure. Pete, just before coming to the graveyard, offered to relieve Jack of his burden. He was an athletic Negro. Joe readily agreed to be transferred to Pete's care. As they came up to the corner of the graveyard, the would-be ghost raised up. Pete, as though frightened out of his wits, threw Uncle Joe on the ground hard enough to kill an ordinary Negro, and ran at the top of his speed, leaving poor Joe at the mercy of the ghost. But Joe soon sprang to his feet and made the best time on record. He passed his companions. When they arrived home he was comfortably seated at the fire. They asked him how it was that he made such good time. "Ah, childens, couldn't lay down dar wid dat ghost looking me in de eyes."

In the Blacks in the American West series

Nellie Brown, or The Jealous Wife, with Other Sketches
by Thomas Detter

Shadow and Light: An Autobiography
by Mifflin W. Gibbs

Born to Be
by Taylor Gordon

The Life and Adventures of Nat Love
by Nat Love